"Anne is a passionate therapist and educator who understands how past trauma affects current relationships, including with one's self. Using an anti-oppressive lens, Anne offers a cutting-edge look into how to explore the past to help clients heal in the present. A clinical guide for any therapist who wants to continue dismantling systems to heal future generations, consider *The Colonization of Black Sexualities* essential reading."

—**Kristen Lilla LCSW**, *AASECT Certified Sex Therapist and Educator & Author of* Boxes and How We Fill Them: A Basic Guide to Sexual Awareness

"I'm an older white person and I was hooked from the very first page. The author's writing is beautiful. At one point, she asked the reader to notice what we were feeling in our body. The answer for me was goosebumps. This book provided an abundance of new information for me. It was the most interesting book I have read in a very long time. It was also very practical and I can apply it to my own work as a sex therapist. Truly an exceptional read!"

—**Neil Cannon, PhD, LMFT, CST-S**, *AASECT Certified Sex Therapist & Supervisor, Denver, CO, USA*

"Anne Mauro delivers an engaging and informative read that exemplifies the need for Black voices and experiences to be heard, understood, and valued in the mental health and sex therapy fields. Her work is a triumph in decolonizing and unsettling sexuality and is a must read for all those working toward healing, relearning, and liberation."

—**Dr. Roger Kuhn, (Poarch Creek), CST, LMFT**, *activist, artist, writer*

"Dr Anne Mauro has gifted us with an insightful analysis of how Black sexualities have been colonized and continue to be harmed by sexuality professionals unless we are willing to engage in the necessary work of decolonization and relearning. Flawlessly weaving personal stories, clinical vignettes and scholarship, Dr Mauro guides us through a journey of unlearning, relearning and, ultimately, healing and liberation. This is an essential book for sexuality professionals and, indeed, all healthcare providers and educators."

—**Alex Iantaffi, PhD, MS, SEP, CST, LMFT**, *Author of* Gender Trauma: Healing Cultural, Social and Historical Gendered Trauma *and President of the Minnesota Association for Marriage and Family Therapy*

"A warm invitation to a Foucauldian 1619 Project revealing the sexual healing possibilities when American settler sex and gender colonizing power is empathically brought to consciousness in the sexual lives of our clients, their therapists and our nation."

—**Doug Braun-Harvey**, *The Harvey Institute, San Diego, California, USA*

"A must read text for students and scholars of critical sexuality studies and sexuality professionals committed to self-growth and healing the impact of oppressive forces. This work is essential for contextualizing Black sexualities and presents an opportunity to reflect on the impact of colonization and cis-hetero-patriarchy on sexualities and increase sexual multiepistemic literacy. This work contributes to the depatriarchalization of sexuality studies and provides foundational content for the history of Black sexuality."

—**Zelaika Hepworth Clarke, PhD, MSW, MEd**, *eroticologist and cofounder of the decolonial sexuality studies program at Goddard College, Washington, USA*

The Colonization of Black Sexualities

Anne Mauro invites therapists to look through a historical lens to view how the harmful effects of colonization and white supremacy impact their Black client's sexuality in the modern day.

Written from her unique position as a sex therapist and bi-racial Black woman, Mauro believes that by relearning the history of sexual trauma on African American bodies, clinicians can better assess their client's intergenerational trauma and inform their work and practice. Chapters address how the patriarchy was an agent in colonization, the impact of colonization on ethnosexuality, slavery, and sexuality, ethnosexual historical traumas and their impact on modern-day American sexual behavior, and the continuing effects of sexual violence and sexual health disparities in young Black women and girls. With reflective questions woven throughout, the final chapter guides the therapist through clinical practices meant for grounding, healing, and the promotion of authenticity within this work. It offers tangible insights into dismantling oppressive practices and integrating the material into the reader's personal and professional lives.

The book is essential reading for students of gender studies, human sexuality, and race studies, as well as all mental health professionals, such as sex therapists, marriage and family therapists, and clinical social workers.

Anne Mauro is dually certified as an AASECT certified sex therapist and sexuality educator, licensed relationship therapist, and AAMFT and AASECT clinical supervisor.

Leading Conversations on Black Sexualities and Identities
Series editors
James C. Wadley

Leading Conversations on Black Sexualities and Identities aims to stimulate sensitive conversations and teachings surrounding Black sexuality. Written by academics and practitioners who have dedicated their work to the distinctive sexual and relational experiences of persons of African descent, the series aims to provoke an enhanced understanding throughout the field of sexology and identify educational and clinical strategies for change. Amplifying issues and voices often minimalized and marginalized, this series is a continuation and expansion of inquiry and advocacy upon the complexities and nuances of relational negotiation, identity affirmation, critical discourse, and liberated sexual expression.

Titles in the series:

Internalized Homonegativity Among Same Gender Loving Black Men
An Exploration of Truths
by P. Ryan Grant

Sexual Health and Black College Students
Exploring the Sexual Milieu of HBCUs
Naomi M. Hall

Black Women, Intersectionality, and Workplace Bullying
Intersecting Distress
Leah P. Hollis

The Colonization of Black Sexualities
A Clinical Guide to Relearning and Healing
Anne Mauro

The Colonization
of Black Sexualities

A Clinical Guide to Relearning
and Healing

Anne Mauro

Routledge
Taylor & Francis Group
NEW YORK AND LONDON

First published 2024
by Routledge
605 Third Avenue, New York, NY 10158

and by Routledge
4 Park Square, Milton Park, Abingdon, Oxon, OX14 4RN

Routledge is an imprint of the Taylor & Francis Group, an informa business

Library of Congress Cataloging-in-Publication Data
Names: Mauro, Anne, author.
Title: The colonization of Black sexualities : a clinical guide to relearning and healing / Anne Mauro.
Description: New York, NY : Routledge, Taylor & Francis Group, 2024. | Series: Leading conversations on Black sexualities and identities | Includes bibliographical references and index.
Identifiers: LCCN 2023007420 (print) | LCCN 2023007421 (ebook) | ISBN 9781032233680 (hardback) | ISBN 9781032233697 (paperback) | ISBN 9781003276951 (ebook)
Subjects: LCSH: African Americans—Psychology. | African Americans—Sexual behavior. | Sex—United States—History. | Generational trauma—United States.
Classification: LCC E185.625 .M345 2024 (print) | LCC E185.625 (ebook) | DDC 306.7089/96073—dc23/eng/20230308
LC record available at https://lccn.loc.gov/2023007420
LC ebook record available at https://lccn.loc.gov/2023007421

ISBN: 978-1-032-23368-0 (hbk)
ISBN: 978-1-032-23369-7 (pbk)
ISBN: 978-1-003-27695-1 (ebk)

DOI: 10.4324/9781003276951

Typeset in Times New Roman
by Apex CoVantage, LLC

Contents

Foreword

I believe that Dr. Anne Mauro and I met several years ago through mutual colleagues who insisted that we meet one another. Even though we live in different geographical regions (Anne lives in the Pacific Northwest and I live in Philadelphia), our colleagues suggested that our professional paths should cross. Both Anne and I are BIPOC sexuality therapists and educators, and it may have been that our mutual colleagues wanted us to meet because of that shared identity.

I'm not quite sure if our first encounter was in person at a conference, a workshop, or online, but I could instantly tell that Anne was different. What made my experience with Anne different than some of the other meetings I've had with other professionals is that Anne is insightful, courageous, and passionate about being authentic. When we first met, it felt like she was free and untethered to conventional ideologies and norms that hold professionals bound. It may have been that her insight and courage were developed and enhanced by her experiences as a bi-racial person and toggling between familial and relational identities.

During several conversations that we've had over the years, Anne shared some of the personal elements she offered to us in her writing. She and I have talked about race and ethnic identities, parenting, partnering, self-care, professionalism, and being authentic in spaces that suggest that we present otherwise. In our discussions, Anne revealed several professional challenges over the years, and how she has managed and overcame them over a variety of contexts. What's interesting is that Anne never wavers in being herself and because of this, others are inspired to do the same. When she agreed to share herself and work on decolonization with our community, I was moved because I knew that we would get the best of our field from Anne's scholarship, clinical work, and leadership.

What's profound and compelling about what Dr. Anne Mauro gives to us is that this book fills a tremendous hole that we have in the fields of sexology and sex therapy. As a field, we need to engage in more meaningful conversations about decolonization and the identities that each of us maintain that clings to elements of white supremacy. My colleagues and I have spent years talking about diversity, equity, inclusion, and access, and we sometimes struggle with putting our finger on the "in moment" experiences of wrestling with systemic oppression and our own internal confrontation with authenticity.

Reflections

How do I confront internalized white supremacy when I am around BIPOC professionals?

How do I confront white supremacy when I am the only person of color in a particular space?

In this book, Anne uses her own experiences as a bi-racial woman and meticulously guides us to question and discuss who we are as professionals, as individuals, and as a field. This book leads a wonderful discussion about Black sexualities and identities because it addresses the complexities of how we define ourselves as people and professionals and calls into question how we present to those around us. Dr. Mauro offers us a path to enlightenment and emancipation through decolonization. Her work is a literary gift that frees us from our limited understanding about sexuality, mental health, and wellness. Indeed, Anne is a generational talent who gives our field of sex therapy and education an invitation to move beyond its colonization into more spaces and moments of authenticity.

Elegua

Gratitude

I am indebted to the academics and scholars that have shared wisdom and offered me a foundation to grow and stand. Kim Tallbear, Reid Gustafson, Imani Perry, Resmaa Menekeem, Zelaika S. Hepworth Clarke Carnegie, Roger Kuhn, James Wadley, and so many more.

My children: Viviana, thank you for sacrificing your mother for her work. Vincent, thank you for staying with me in your death.

My planet, ancestors, beloved departed, and all that surrounds, supports, and sustains me, I draw strength from you.

Content disclaimer

Please consider this book mentions sexual traumas of people of all ages by visiting sexual violence past and present. Tend to yourself as needed. I am reminding you that language is constantly revolving and evolving. The data, literature, and research on sexualities come from a very white/cis/hetero/racist/monogamist, and amatonormative place. Although there has been intention to avoid perpetuating those standards of language here, at times, especially when discussing the colonial past, it can be difficult. I intentionally capitalize B for Black and I for Indigenous and lower the w for white and c for christianity to bring awareness to how we use language and words to elevate and oppress. I would like to dismantle the systemic power whiteness and cis-hetero-patriarchy holds in our words and meaning-making. With forced assimilation, many words that represented the sexualities of African and Indigenous people, as they knew it, are missing from our vocabulary. Please considerer that there is a gap between history and modern praxis. I do not have the answers of how to bridge this gap. I'm opening the door for further exploration of anti-colonial practices within the field of sexology. To celebrate those that I have built my knowledge on, I will write out the title of their works in gratitude.

DOI: 10.4324/9781003276951-1

Key terms

Folx: an inclusive way to say folks.

Elegua

In West Africa, the Yoruba people held the foundation to what would become many different religions within the African diaspora. With the transatlantic slave trade, Africans were being transported to ports not only in the Americas but also places such as Cuba, Brazil, and Haiti. When enslaved Africans were brought to what is now known as North America, they were forbidden from practicing their religion and customs. Many were forced to adopt the religion of the settlers. Some enslaved folx kept their religion secret from their masters and other watchful eyes, even disguising their practices as their oppressors' religion by syncretizing deities (orishas) for saints, keeping it alive for some of us today. In modern days, when suggestions of Voodoo, Santeria, or other derivatives of the Yoruba religion surface, it is pathologized, stigmatized, and can be seen as maleficent. The same hiding, stigma, and fear seen around these non-Christian religions are similar to stigma and fear that can be seen around sex. In their dissertation, *Coming to My Senses: A Decolonizing Autoethnographic Exploration of Osunality*, Dr. Zelaika Hepworth Clark speaks of the importance of "Sexual multiepistemic literacy." They define it as, "A theory of knowledge that acknowledges the existence of more than one way of understanding knowledge, even if it is understood to be contradictory" (Hepworth Clark, 2015, p. 26). Some of us struggle with things that are contrary to what we are taught and believe. Dr. Zel encourages us to "make available multiple ways of understanding sexual knowledge and interpretations about issues surrounding sexualities outside the westerncentric paradigms" (Hepworth Clark, 2015, p. 1). Sexual multiepistemic literacy invites other ways of knowing, believing, and seeing our sexuality. With the imposition of colonialism, christian supremacy, and white supremacy, as a culture, we are accustomed to one "right" way of being and knowing. When it comes to sex, the "right" and "proper" way to be sexual is intrinsically tied to settler sexuality. Dr. Zel challenges us to open and expand our thinking beyond western paradigms. I want to bring that challenge into this space so that you can open yourself to other more expansive ways than the ones we, especially Americans, are accustomed to. Due to christianization and white supremacy, many ways of understanding the world have been outshadowed or shamed out of existence. Let's set the tone by reminding ourselves that there are ways of being beyond the dominant discourse of christianity and western centric ways of being. If possible, with your current circumstances, I invite you to say aloud, "There are more ways to know. There are more ways to understand. There are more ways to listen. There are more ways to be." If you were able to recite the words, how did it feel? Did you believe them? Did you resist it? Did it bring hope or fear? We as a culture are aware of other religions, such as Islam, Hinduism, and Judaism; however, far too many other belief systems have been cast to the shadows. Santeria, also known as La Regla de Ocha or Regla Lucumí is one of them. In this Yoruba-based religion, there is the creator, the genderless Olodumare, and many spirit-like deities called orishas—with each orisha possessing their own unique power and deficits. In an attempt to dismantle christian supremacy in my writing, I have named each chapter after an orisha. This chapter is named after the Orisha, my warrior, Elegua. He is known to represent beginnings. Before a santerx (santero) begins a ritual or ceremony in La Regla de Ocha, they request the consent of Elegua. He is called upon first, as he possesses the key to communicate with the other orishas, and the ability to open or block our path. I would like to express gratitude to Elegua for opening this path for both of us.

Positionality

I would like to introduce myself to you, so you are aware of my positionality. I am an American Association Sex Educators Counselors and Therapist (AASECT) certified sex therapist, certified sex educator, and AASECT and American Association of Marriage and Family Therapy (AAMFT) clinical supervisor. I am a Bi-racial Black woman born during the Loving Generation. The Loving Generation are typically folx of Black and white descent born between the anti-miscegenation case *Loving vs Virginia* in 1967 through the early 1980s. I was baptized Lutheran, attended some catholic school, and I am an aboricha, which is a devotee of the orishas. I was born to a white mother (second-generation Italian and English and third-generation Swedish), who raised me as a single parent, and gave me her last name—the name of my southern Italian grandfather. His mother, who only spoke an Italian dialect called grimaldese, came to the states, an underaged girl, for an arranged marriage to a man she never met. My African American father, who shares the last name of our descendant's first enslaver, remained incarcerated for the first 38 years of my life. Our people were enslaved in Alabama prior to moving to Iowa during the Great Migration. At least three generations of my kin on each side have lived in the Pacific Northwest (PNW). I think what is important to acknowledge is that I was raised by a single white mother in predominantly white spaces. This differentiates my positionality from other Black folx who have two Black parents or from the home of another mixed person who had a Black parent and/or culture vibrating in their homes. When writing this I questioned if I could write this piece due to my proximity to whiteness. This insecurity of "am I Black enough to write this" has been reinforced by interactions I have had with others.

An example of this is during 2020, when the global pandemic and the social uprisings took their course in tandem, a sexuality professional started a group for People of Color to support each other. At the time, I was grieving. Grieving over the loss of multiple white relatives that I had separated from during the Trump administration. I was isolated working from my home office. I was a single parent with a seven-year-old doing distance learning from home. Our only social interactions were happening at the grocery store. The regular smiling faces of the grocers looked weary, and I was tired. Their once smiles were now covered in masks. My work as a clinician really morphed into something I did not recognize. It had changed so much, from doing sex therapy with high-functioning clients, to doing crisis interventions, and facilitating hospitalizations with these same clients. So naturally when I saw the opportunity to be in community with other POCs doing the same work, I jumped on it and sent a reply to join the group. The response caused a sinking in my heart and a pit in my stomach. It said, "Hi, Anne. We decided to use this space for just Black sexuality professionals. I will let you know if we open another space for POC." It's been made clear to me by other folx, that my Blackness is not enough Blackness to be Black. This, naturally, exacerbated my imposter syndrome, and I have struggled with if I should write this piece titled, *The Colonization of Black Sexualities: A clinical guide to relearning and healing*. Ijeoma Oluo speaks to this distinction of identifying as Black when born to a white mother when she says, "I will say, I am half Nigerian," or "I am mixed-race Black," or "my mother is white." But I am not white—I'm not even half-white. My mother is white. I am Black" (Oluo, 2021). No matter how we identify, in many ways, we are just the projection of the limited perceptions of race and culture. These projections can freeze parts of ourselves that have internalized others' perceptions. Oluo obviously has had to offer an explanation for how she looks and for how she identifies. I have granted others the power to identify me many times. This is one reason I try to move through my work, allowing others to identify themselves. My experience of coloniality has been informed by the dichotomous rival of colonizer and colonized that lives within me. I wholeheartedly acknowledge my proximity to whiteness as a writer and speaker of Black sexuality.

My mother and I started out in 1980 in government housing in what is called Rat City (White Center) a suburb of Seattle. We had food stamps when they used to come in what looked like a little rectangular paper coupon book. I still remember the feel of those paper pages, and the sound it made when you ripped out a little page from the book. My great uncle who lived up the hill, on Roxbury, where the *real* houses were, would share his powdered milk and gigantic block of government cheese with us each month. My mother continued education, joined the military, and pursued many professional achievements that offered upward mobility throughout my lifespan increasing resources available to me. I identify as multicultural, cis, woman, queer (with hetero privilege being a single parent), visibly able-bodied, with a back injury that causes chronic pain, femme with light-skinned privilege, that was made and raised in the PNW. I live and profit from the unceded lands of the Coast Salish Peoples. Specifically, the *Duwamish* and *Puyallup* tribes. I acknowledge the direct correlation to this original land theft and the continued genocide and sexual violence toward Black, Indigenous, Latinx, people of color, and culture, sexual minorities, and gender expansive folx. It is my hope that as we continue to resist, dismantle, re-learn, and re-exist, that we become good ancestors to the children born long after we are gone. My ancestors (egun), orishas, guides, and spirits that tend to my well-being have been invited to this space. I welcome you to invite anyone or anything you would like to support you on this literary journey.

There were times when I sat down to write this, I wanted to weep. This work is hard, and sometimes I feel like I am suffering through the writing. I had to ask for an extension on this project deadline because the words wouldn't appear on the page. More than once I have been frozen. Sitting in my chair in front of my screen—eyes moistening. A growing sensation in my throat feeling like someone or something has their hand around it, and the grip is tightening. I've heard the throat is symbolic of speaking your truth. I wonder to myself, "Is this my truth activating this part of me? Or, is it the ancestors, the dead, the unseen creating this constriction?" I have read, heard, and written about the atrocities that so many people have faced. Sometimes I feel as if I am holding some of them inside. Alive, here with me, in my body. I looked to my own ancestors while doing this work. One in particular, I felt has carried me through this writing project, Babe Lavender. I could feel her presence lingering in space, holding me in time. The more I tuned into these sensations, the more I felt she would interact with me with subtle synchronicities. Small things, like, I strangely stumbling across lavender gum or being given a small tube of lavender lotion after just thinking of her. After mentioning Babe Lavender's name to my daughter as we were dinning at a restaurant, the server approached and I asked him what drink he would recommend, and he says, "Lavender Lemonade." The day after I turned in my first draft to the editor, my uncle and his partner gifted me lavender soap without they themselves making any connection to it. All of these scenarios feel more than coincidences. These messages from a person who had transitioned long before I was born felt like she was connecting with me. You and I both could easily dismiss all of these "signs," but when I turn inward, and I am able to connect with the deepest part of my knowing, I know Babe Lavender is here, and interacting with me in the physical world. I have tried to make this connection with other ancestors from her generation and beyond and nothing feels like what I feel between her and I. One distant relative, Lazarus, has been on my mind for some time. He does not speak to me, certainly not like Babe Lavender, and not like other transitioned people I have sensed before. I do not feel him in my body. Yet, I think of him often, and I'm left with so many questions about his story. His father was a second-generation white enslaver named John. John was never married; however, birthed one son in 1829, Lazarus. The different documentation of Lazarus identifies as Black or mulatto. Frustratingly, I have yet to find any documentation of his mother. I looked through my family records reviewing the "Slave Inhabitants" documentation detailing the ages of all of the unnamed enslaved people John had in 1860, five years prior to slavery being abolished. At that time, Lazarus would have been 31 years old. The document shows that at that time, John owned 17 people, the youngest being four months old and the oldest just 35. None of them was old enough to be Lazarus' mother. The more I look, the more questions I have. Why didn't John do what was customary at the time and marry a white woman? Why didn't John have any other children, especially, with a white woman? How did he treat his enslaved Black son? How could he enslave a man that was just years older than his own son? Why did he own so many children? Long after he watched his own Black son become an adult. Out of the 17 people he owned, 11 were children under the age of 15. Again, I think to myself, "What was he doing with all of these children. Where is Lazarus' mother? What was the story erased from traceable records? When and how did she lose connection with her son?" I'm left thinking of her and countless other untraceable people who had been used for sex, abused, separated from kinships, mistreated, and discarded—unable to speak their truth. Leaving no traceable evidence for us to unearth now. I go back to noticing this tightness in my throat and ask myself again, "Is this my tightness or theirs? Do I need to say this now? What do they want to say?" I cry. The sorrow runs deep. Despair and disbelief crippling my ability to type. My bones are heavy again. I'm holding weight that is heavier than my own. I am discouraged with questions like, how are we, as Americans, here now? Why aren't we as a collective in the country seeing the connections between the harm of the past and what we feel now? I want the pain in my throat to release. I bring in cool clear breath through my nose and send it to my throat with acknowledgment of the burden it's been carrying. I relax my shoulders. I remember to breath and I continue to write. Moving through this work, I continue to pause and reflect on what messages I am receiving. I encourage you to do the same while you read this. As I have demonstrated for you above, this is an invitation to paying attention to your somatic cues, the settling and unsettling of your body.

It is a difficult task to re-learn history, uncover injustices, and see the pain on both a micro- and macrolevel. In my studies on the subject of sexuality and colonization, I have felt so much. It brings heaviness. At times, I felt like I was carrying the pain of my ancestors, and it made my joints ache. There is a challenge in honoring the dead while teaching the horrors they have experienced. The fear of disrespecting them or re-traumatizing, you can come on so strong, I think that it was freezes me in place. This manuscript is centering Black sexuality in the critical analysis of colonization. Daina Ramey Berry and Leslie Harris, editors of *Sexuality and Slavery: Reclaiming Intimate Histories in the Americas* write, "The balance between creating respectful portrayals without reinscribing exploitation represents one of the many challenges of this work" (Berry & Harris, 2018, p. 4). I had to trust this process and trust that you are here to hear this and that you will take the breaks you need, when you need them—equal parts of truth-telling and healing needs to happen simultaneously. This book is an attempt to offer you both and to provide you with some clinical considerations. I encourage you to pay attention to your body, as I am to mine. Witnessing it through this journey and tending to yourself with somatic care and love.

If you're questioning what all of this has to do with modern-day sexuality, sex therapy, and healing, let me offer the basic tenant of Sexological Systems Theory which says, "The development of one's sexuality is the result of biological and psychological processes that are enacted within a socio-cultural context, which, in turn, shapes its expression" (Jones et al., 2011, p. 128). This theory provides room for examining the historical forces that impact on our sexual development. I argue that the historical sexual traumas that will be mentioned in this text shape and inform the sociocultural context of today. It is this impact that is heavily influencing modern-day sexualities. We will discuss this theory later in the last chapter.

Expanding the expanded Addressing Model

Before we go further, I want to offer a tool that is helpful to utilize when examining positionality. I used it as somewhat of a guide to tell you about myself above. It can be challenging to see how our positionality informs our views of the world and how autocolonization has infiltrated our daily lives and thinking. Walter D. Mignolo writes, "Coloniality is more difficult to see. Modernity's storytelling hides it. But it is felt, it is felt by people who do not fit the celebratory frames and expectations of modernity" (Mignolo, 2016). A good start to anti-colonial work is acknowledging that our unique lens is insidiously inseparable from western and eurocentric ways of seeing. Due to autocolonization, it can be difficult to see what we are blind to. I compare this to the movie *the Matrix*. We don't know that we are plugged into a false reality until we get unplugged. Then, it takes time to grapple with the newfound realities we are faced with. When I started teaching Case Consultation to graduate-level interns, I was happy to see the students were accustomed to using the Addressing Model developed by Pamela Hays (2008) to assist them in seeing how their own positionality is interacting with their clients'. It offers a framework for viewing and understanding the complexities of how our lens shapes how we see the world and gives us an idea of where our blind spots may be. It's a tool designed for clinicians to open their eyes to areas of oppression, power, and privilege in the therapy room. This is done by exploring whether an individual is considered to be a "target," from oppressed and marginalized groups or "agent," the privileged groups, in each of the following categories: age, developmental disabilities, acquired disabilities, religion, ethnicity, sexual orientation, socioeconomic status, Indigenous group membership, nationality, and gender. If a therapist completes the Addressing Model for their own positionality and that of their clients', the therapist is offered a broader understanding of how their positionality is converging with their clients' positionality; thus, creating an intricate web holding all the overlapping identities. I brought in the expanded Addressing Model into the Case Consultation course I was teaching. In addition to the original Addressing Model, the Expanded Addressing Model allows us to also reflect on "Dogma (beliefs; philosophy; politics), the generational influences, cognitive and psychological disabilities, giftedness, spiritual orientation, geographical region, rural, urban, suburban, exurban, national origin, relationship status, and genetics" such as "biologically related to parents." I particularly liked the addition of having the option to identify a person as one, two, or more than one race, "uni-, bi-, and multiracial."

Each week, as students presented on cases in the class, we teased apart the model as we continued to explore and integrate other meaningful pieces when creating our own version of the expanded Addressing Model. My students, Morris, Ciera Coyan, Amanda Routledge, Jen Davis, Ross Kling, and myself added our own parts and dissected others. It was my then student, and now supervisee, Ciera, that started implementing within all of her case conceptualizations what structural oppressions can arise in all domains of the ADDRESSING Model and how that may be impacting the "in-room power dynamics" to use Ciera's words, she asks, "are the in-the room power dynamics 'equitable' or is someone holding more power in this domain (i.e., age, race, gender)?" For example, if you are examining the Age domain of the Addressing Model, you would ask yourself, "how is agism showing up in the therapy room and in each of our lives." Then we can be curious about how our unique positionality is interacting with our clients' and to be mindful and intentional about the power dynamics as we proceed with treatment.

It's no surprise now that America has protected and empowered white-hetero-cis-sexist and racist frameworks. By having identities that are seen as valued, your ranking on our unspoken societal hierarchy rises. In her book, *Caste: The origins of our discontents*, author Isabel Wilkerson believes that an American caste system keeps people in a "fixed place" with an "artificial hierarchy" that "goes against human's desire to be free" (Wilkerson, 2020). Through the colonial assimilation processes, we have all fallen victim to autocolonization, and now it's time to wake up. White supremacy only wants it one way. What it sees as the "normal way" the way that maintains a racial divide, dictates standards of beauty, normalizes specific sex acts, while pathologizing others. Historically, our theories and methods have been used to harm marginalized groups. The medical model is built using the blood of BILPOC, gender expansive, and queer folx. Since the dominant discourse is able to create these structures of knowing which is enveloped as "common sense," it is important that we now make room for other ways of being, learning, teaching, and therapizing using a multiepistemic lens (Hepworth Clark, 2015).

As I alluded to before, my research is centered on the colonization of what we now call America by the English settlers. In Chapter 1, you will spend some time critically analyzing patriarchy, as this was an established system prior to the English colonizing North America. This section assists you, as the reader, in understanding how patriarchy was an agent in colonization, globalization, and neoliberalism. Imani Perry author of *Vexing Things: On Gender and Liberation* contends that patriarchy's formation took three judicial forms: sovereignty, property, and personhood (Perry, 2018). Perry argues that the formation of patriarchy begins in the Enlightenment era as taxonomies are born to help understand the world around us. The need to have order in social relationships helped foster a hierarchy of personhood, man, woman, freeman, negro, and slave. Personhood and citizenship were tied directly to property. In order to protect said property, men were motivated to join political society to protect said property. This social order, with men on top, offered domination of women and those considered "nonpersons." The christian religion placed the father in the position of power to care and rule over his family, thus mimicking ruling powers. Under the man, the women's role was to be "virtuous in domestic responsibilities and religious obligations" (Perry, 2018). Enslaved people had no legal recognition. "Personhood and patriarchy became a way to determine who counted and who did not amount the human, and for what purpose when it came to various social and political concerns" (Perry, 2018). The coercive powers at hand were sure to make nonpersons appear deviant and savage in terms of gender and sexuality and encouraged one to be "civilized" (Perry, 2018). Order was established by means of legality, with at times, harsh punishment for those that broke the established rules on gender and sexuality.

Chapter 2 covers ethnosexuality. Ethnosexuality is a term coined by Joane Nagel (2000) in the journal article "Ethnicity and Sexuality" to describe the intersection of race/ethnicity and sexuality. This chapter examines the impact of colonization on ethnosexuality with emphasis on Black-bodied sexuality. Nagel writes, "No ethnic boundary is more sexualized, surveilled, and scrutinized in US society than the color line dividing blacks and whites" (p. 122). In order to understand ethnosexuality, I plan to discuss white body supremacy and how it continues to be projected onto to Black sexualities. The works of Resmaa Menekeem, Robin DiAngelo, and Layla Said will be used to solidify the understanding of white dominant discourse and its effects. Anti-miscegenation, the prevention of races coming together in intimate ways, will also be discussed here. Nagel (2000) wrote that we need to

> expose the sexualized foundations of ethnicity by examining the ways in which the rule breaking, policing, and punishment of sexual deviants serves both to challenge and to reinforce racial, ethnic, and nationalist boundaries and hegemonies and to strengthen ethnosexual regimes.
>
> (p. 118)

A greater understanding of American miscegenation will offer the reader an enhanced insight into American ethnosexuality through interracial sexual violence.

Chapter 3 is an in depth look into the sexualities of the enslaved Africans and African Americans. With the transatlantic slave trade, Africans became the largest minority group, quickly outnumbering the Indigenous population. Although laws were in place prohibiting sexual contact between races, we have insurmountable evidence proving that these laws were in place to protect white people—more specifically, white women (Solomon, 2017). Solomon writes, "rape and sexual violence became another way for whites to reify dominance and control over blacks." In the book *The Half Has Never Been Told*, Edward Baptist writes, "Slavery's frontier was a white man's sexual playground" (Baptist, 2014, p. 238). This chapter examines some historical sexual traumas of children and adults of all genders. Highlighting not only the sadistic past of individuals but also the system that created the culture of abuse.

Chapter 4 offers an introduction to understanding racialized sexual trauma and its effects on individuals and communities to the present day. In his book *My Grandmother's Hands: Racialized Trauma and the Pathway to Mending our Hearts and Bodies*, Resmaa Menekeem offers a guide in looking at how the historical trauma of our ancestors are impacting us today. He writes, "Our very bodies house the unhealed dissonance and trauma of our ancestors" (p. 10). This chapter will explore how the historical sexual trauma lives on in our bodies also. Menekeem shows us that it is a combination of "genes, history, culture, laws, and family" that impacts the trauma stored in Black bodies. He goes on to say, "That trauma then becomes the unconscious lens through which they view all of the current experiences" (p. 13). Even sexual experiences. Menekeem refers to this trauma in the body as a "wordless story." We can't tap into it with words, thoughts, or cognitions. Repeatedly, it keeps getting passed down generation after generation. The chapter assists the reader in identifying some ethnosexual historical traumas and their impact on modern-day American sexual behavior and draw connections to present-day Black bodies.

Chapter 5 provides information on current themes and trends in present-day American Sexuality that's etiology can be traced back to colonization. The Missing and Murdered Indigenous women, girls, and Two Spirit (MMI-WG2S+) epidemic and the need for the #MeToo movement are desperate signals of the continuation of sexual violence from our colonial past. According to a 2014 *study*, about 22 percent of Black women reported being raped and 41 percent experienced other forms of *sexual violence*. For every Black woman who reports her rape, *at least* 15 Black women do not report (Bureau of Justice Statistics Special Report, Hart & Rennison, 2003. U.S. Department of Justice). Black women have the highest disparities in prenatal care, and they are more likely to die during childbirth. Black babies die at three times that of their white counterparts; however, their mortality is increased, if they are birthed by a Black doctor. Black babies also have a lower birth weight, greater chances of childhood obesity, early menses, and cervical cancer.

Critical analysis of American history can assist us in understanding how we got here today.

In Chapter 6, I discuss clinical considerations moving forward. I will discuss how we can implement de-colonial practices in ourselves and in our work. Nkiru Nzegwu definition of Osun is "the divinity of fertility, wealth, joy, sensuality and childbirth, protector of women and giver of children to barren women" (p. 258). She embodies sexuality and pleasure. We sex educators have long been aware of the lack of pleasure-based sexuality curriculum. At its core, Osunality "encourages the treatment of sexual pleasuring and enjoyment as of optional importance" (p. 261). Unlike patriarchal frameworks, this matriarchal lens does not negate the sexuality of those that do not identify as woman. Osun herself takes the form of a peacock, not a peahen, but a peacock; thus, another demonstration of the fluidity in gender. After we have done some learning and un-learning, it will be time to apply the information into clinical practice. This chapter will guide the therapists through clinical practices meant for more healing through the promotion of pleasure.

This is a gentle reminder to move at your own pace and take the breaks you need. You're invited to stretch your body, take a deep breath, or maybe lightly hum.

1   Obatala

Amatonormative—a term coined by Elizabeth Brake "to describe the widespread assumption that everyone is better off in an exclusive, romantic, long-term coupled relationship, and that everyone is seeking such a relationship" (Brake, 2012).

Many of us have a general idea of what patriarchy is. One simple definition of patriarchy I found "is that of an old, common structure that organizes gender into a binary, hierarchical system" (Stimpson, 2020). Patriarchy created systemic privileges that maintain a white, cis-hetero-male-dominated society while simultaneously discriminating marginalized communities like women, trans, gender expansive, BILPOCC, and folx with disabilities. Before we get into the history of the formation of patriarchy here in "America," I would like you to take a pause and reflect on the following questions:

Reflection

What does patriarchy mean to you?
When did you first learn about it?
When was the first time you heard the term "cis-hetero-patriarchy?"
How do you see patriarchy and race intersecting?
What do you know about the origins of patriarchy in the United States?
What did your family of origin teach you about patriarchy?
Why do you think we are adhering to a patriarchal system now?
How has patriarchy impacted you?
How has it impacted your education and work?

I think in order to better understand modern patriarchy, we need to examine the historical context to truly grasp the suppression of marginalized folx. How people assigned female at birth (AFAB), Black, Indigenous, gender expansive, and anyone other than white/cis-het have been treated in this country can give an understanding of the superiority and oppression that is insidiously intertwined in our culture. For the past couple of years, my research and studies have centered around the colonization of what we now call "North America"

DOI: 10.4324/9781003276951-2

and its impacts on modern-day American sexuality. The three populations I have focused on have been Native American (Indigenous), enslaved Africans and African Americans, the English settlers, and white people. Before starting this work, I didn't have an interest in history. Early in life, I never really enjoyed learning about history at all. Looking back now, I wonder how I even graduated from public education with such limited knowledge of history. This started to change when in my postgraduate work, I simultaneously grappled to understand two phenomena: the Missing and Murdered Indigenous Women, Girl, and 2 Spirit+ epidemic and anti-miscegenation. MMIWGT2S+ will be discussed later in Chapter 5 and anti-miscegenation will be discussed in Chapter 2. When researching on both, each one led me to the same place: colonization. Looking at these historical events through a sexological lens is when my work started to simmer in this intersection between race/ethnicity and sexuality: ethnosexuality. I knew that a lot of history was falsified, but even with that knowing, I experienced heartache while doing this work, partly from being so disillusioned by the romanticized history I was taught. From the overt to the subtle shifts in the narrative, I grew frustrated in how many others were still in the matrix unable to see the truth in front of us. I mean, it makes sense. This is the same history that my grandparents learned. Singing the same songs my daughter was taught when she attended private christian school. From my pain and part empowerment, I made the decision to offer my child the truth. This meant challenging the curriculum she was taught and offering us both a communal re-learning and truth-telling. Many holidays my child (whom I affectionately call my kiddo) would come home with problematic worksheets, songs, or I would actually witness harmful teachings and messaging when I would participate in activities at the school. These inaccuracies offered me a gentle opportunity to say, "Oh, no, baby. That's not exactly how that went down," or "I'm not sure we should be celebrating this event/person. Can I tell you why I think that?" There have been several times that I addressed my kiddo's teacher or principal with my concerns. My kiddo since has transferred to a more progressive school that teaches much closer to the truth. Sadly, this is not just a concern with K–12, I have also had to address parallel concerns as adjunct faculty in higher education. So, naturally, we have all become disillusioned by the falsified stories that are imposed on us. All of us at some points have adhered to a narrative that was created to uplift some and diminish others.

This book is a consolidation of some of this unearthing of truths and untruths of the history of American sexuality. It's hard to recognize unless we are unplugged from the falsified narrative. I am going to discuss some hard historical facts and invite you to continue your individual and our collective healing. As we move through the chapters in this book, I will offer you tools to incorporate healing from these historical sexual traumas in your work. I hope that this will encourage you to move into anti-colonial spaces with the intention of tending to yourself throughout.

Since a foundational piece of colonization is patriarchy, I will spend some time looking at some ways patriarchy has been imposed, as it was an established system prior to the English colonizing North America. I think the best place to start this journey is with defining settler colonialism. There have been many colonizers throughout history, including the Spanish, French, Dutch, Portuguese, and British. For the sake of this book, we will be concentrating on the English colonization of North America. In the book, *Native America and the Question of Genocide*, Alex Alverez wrote, "Settler colonialism is predicated on the notion of destroying Indigenous populations to make room for the incoming waves of settlers who want to create a replica of their home society" (Alvarez, 2014). The Manifest Destiny and The Doctrine of Discovery offered justification for the land theft of non-christians and promoted the continued growth of christian supremacy, sexual violence, and genocide of Indigenous peoples. My American Association of Marriage and Family Therapy (AAMFT) mentor, Alex Iantaffi writes in his book *Gender Trauma: Healing Cultural, Social, and Historical Gendered Trauma*, "If Indigenous people could be considered as less than human as non-Christians, then their land could be taken, and they could be enslaved, abused, and/or forcibly made to assimilate into the new settler colonial state" (Iantaffi, 2021, p. 24). Iantaffi reminds us that "Settler colonialism doesn't just happen at one point in history; it is an ongoing project that continuously undermines Indigenous identities, culture and sovereignty" (Iantaffi, 2021, p. 22). This premeditated plan, the Settler Colonial Project, was masterfully and successfully executed with fuel from the "settler spirit" to promote onward expansion. This exploration was fed by patriarchy, ignited by colonization, globalization, and neoliberalism.

It was helpful for me to be reminded that patriarchy was a well-established system prior to the English colonizing North America. Imani Perry, in *Vexy Thing: On gender and liberation*, contends that patriarchy's formation took three judicial forms: sovereignty, property, and personhood (Perry, 2018). Perry argues that the formation of patriarchy begins in the Enlightenment era as taxonomies are born to help humans understand the world around them. The need to have order in social relationships unfortunately helped foster a hierarchy to measure a human's status by labeling them as "person, man, woman, freeman, negro, slave." Sadly, personhood and citizenship were tied directly to property, since you could not own land if you were not a "person" or "citizen." In order to protect their property, men were motivated to join political society to ensure protection of land and property. This social order, with men on top, offered domination of women and those considered "nonpersons," which for clarity, is literally everyone else. This helped reinforce that women were not capable of "men's work," education, voting, or land ownership. Over time, the laws collided with this idea that women were incapable of making decisions or being in positions of power due to ability, instead of the reality. Women were not able to participate because of laws, policy, and misconception—not ability. Thus, men continued to profit and benefit from hierarchical power dynamics and women's dependence upon them.

To further reinforce the man in a higher position of power, the christian religion, including influences from Protestantism, placed the father in the position of power to care and rule over his family, thus mimicking ruling powers and God, operating as a commonwealth of ruling powers that protected his kin and property. This ideal of the male/father/patriarch solidified believes that the man is someone who is to be obeyed, as he holds all the power over his wife and children. Under this man, the women's role was to be "virtuous in domestic responsibilities and religious obligations" (Perry, 2018). Children were seen as their father's property—especially "girls." They remained their father's property until they married. Once married, women became the property of their husbands. For women, maintaining these "domestic responsibilities" became a means of survival. With women holding no economic power outside of the household, her economic stability is grounded in being dutiful and faithful to her husband. This established patriarchal power structure that elevated men was perpetuated through American systems and laws.

Patriarchy has been used as a tool to uplift white supremacy. In the book *Native America and the Question of Genocide*, Alvarez writes, "From a colonial mindset, Native populations were usually seen in one of two ways: at best, they were resources to be exploited, and at worst, they were an impediment to be removed" (Alvarez, 2014, p. 56). When they were no longer able to be exploited through mining or plantation labor, "they needed to be relocated or eliminated" (Alvarez, 2014, p. 56). As for the Africans that were transported for slave labor, they as enslaved people had no legal recognition. "Personhood and patriarchy became a way to determine who counted and who did not amount to human, and for what purpose when it came to various social and political concerns" (Perry, 2018). The coercive powers at hand were sure to make nonpersons (Black and Indigenous people) appear deviant and savage in terms of gender and sexuality. They encouraged or better yet forced one to be "civilized" (Perry, 2018). This is so ironic, since settlers were doing what I believe to be highly uncivilized things. Anyway, their mistreatment of anyone other than white cis-men may have been maintained by the cognitive dissonance that had to be present. How else can one reckon with treating other humans so horribly? If settlers could see others as less than, deviant, or nonhuman, the shame and guilt for their true actions would be lessened.

It was through Reid Gustafson's TEDx Talks titled *Hetero-patriarchy and Settler Colonialism* (TEDx, 2019) that I began to understand how patriarchy was established and maintained through early government, law, and policy. Perry writes, "Law is an analytical useful metric for interpreting the creation of modern patriarchy" (Perry, 2018, p. 17). I think it is helpful to call upon Gustafson's analysis to interpret the law's impact on white cis-hetero-patriarchy. Gustafson told his viewers that "Settler colonial assimilation processes looks to impose heteronormative christian monogamy on Indigenous communities in the hope to change sexual practices, familial structures, gender norms, and power dynamics." Many of us are familiar, and if you're not, please look further into: the land theft, removal of Indigenous peoples from their land, prohibitions around Indigenous spiritual practices, genocide, and forced christianity, relocation, eradication, and assimilation (i.e., boarding schools). The treatment the settlers, as a collective, gave to the Indigenous can be a basis of understanding how the enslaved Africans were treated in transport and upon arrival.

Since this section explores patriarchy and its formation, I want to explore Gustafson's work as he offers insight by outlining three Federal Indian Policy Acts: the Dawes/Allotment Act, Indian Reorganization Act, and the Indian Relocation Act. Together, these acts worked to impose heteropatriarchy onto Indigenous bodies, families, and communities. The first act, the 1887 Dawes Act, endowed the president with the authority to survey Indigenous lands, divide it up, and give a specified lot of "surplus land" to Indigenous male "head of household". Any land that was leftover was sold to settlers. With ownership of this land, the Indigenous man became a US citizen. For Indigenous families and tribes that were grounded in matrilineal and matrilocal practices or that distributed their power more equally, this change in power structure initiated a great disruption in Indigenous kinship structures. Iantaffi writes, "Issues like more egalitarian gender roles, matrilineal traditions and adoptions were also seen as undesirable by settlers". (Iantaffi, 2021, p. 24). Gustafson highlights that Indigenous people had to "reorder themselves into families with one man and one woman in order to keep the land they were living on" (Gustafson, 2019). This means that Indigenous people were forced into heteronormative nuclear family structures to survive.

The second act, the 1934 Indian Reorganization Act established western styles of government in tribal councils, where men were the only ones granted positions of power—making all tribal council staff male, "Communities that spread power horizontally had been disrupted" (Gustafson, 2019). This disruption was a benefit to Indigenous men as it granted them more privileges and power in the gender shifts. The 1956 Indian Relocation Act decreased funding going to reservations and increased funds going toward job training and the movement of Indigenous people from reservations to urban centers. This movement into urban areas further forced this nuclear heteronormative lifestyle on Indigenous people; thus, "assimilating Indigenous people into Western capitalism." This is further reinforced by the gendered workforce where men are the pant-wearing, laboring, breadwinners and women the dress-wearing homemakers. We also start to see marketing that reinforces the gender binary with things like colors, blue is for boys and pink if for girls, or food, where steaks are manly and salads are femme. There was extreme power in utilizing consumerism to maintain implicit divide and highlight difference.

When considering the Black experience, as I mentioned before, enslaved people did not have legal recognition. "Personhood and patriarchy became a way to determine who counted and who did not amount to human, and for what purpose when it came to various social and political concerns" (Perry, 2018). Othering became necessary to create a divide between worthy and not. Ironically, what was civilized for whites was to leave their white children an inheritance; however, enslavement was matrilineal and enslaved mothers could not own land to hand down to their children. Their inheritance, even if their father was a white man, may have been enslavement for life (Perry, 2018). Similar to how Indigenous kinships were dismantled, African kinships in America were also undone. Slaveholders were intentionally separated people from the same tribes and families. If Africans could not communicate with each other using the same language, it would be difficult to plan an escape or a rebellion. Therefore, it was common to be separated from those who shared language and customs— leaving the loss of community, tribe, language, country, and disembodiment from their own ancestral land, in turn, disembodiment of the sexual self.

The sexuality of the settlers was imposed upon the Indigenous and Black people. When the settlers arrived to North America, they brought with them a sexuality that would be used as a template for American sexuality for generations to come. To many settlers, sex was seen as something that should be shared by one man and one woman only after they have committed to marriage. After marriage, it was solely intended for procreation. They were so serious about this that if a person was caught using contraception or if one struggled with erectile dysfunction, or infertility, that would be grounds for divorce. The Bastardy Law ensured that if a biological father did not claim his biological child, which they called a bastard or whoreson, that child would not receive his father's inheritance. It should be kept in mind, at the time, women did not work outside the home. Therefore, to become pregnant out of wedlock was not only a shameful act but also a financial burden to the family and possibly community. The Buggery Act (1533) allowed someone to be punished for any "unnatural sexual act against the will of God and Man." For some time, this was the number one infraction brought to the courts. This may have been why it was "later defined by the courts to include only anal penetration and bestiality" (Buggery Act 1533, 2021). Homosexuality, gender expansion, masturbation, anal sex, and premarital sex were strictly forbidden and harshly punished. Communal rules and laws were in place for those who broke the tight sexual boundaries.

Many assume that religion played the largest role in people refraining from sex before marriage. However, an AFAB person's "purity" held their economic value. Since children were under the patriarchal rule, they were under parental supervision until marriage. This led to hypervigilance around sexuality, particularly, monitoring of vulva owner's sexuality. Just like in the Netflix series "Bridgerton," this led to spies keeping a watchful eye on women's chastity. Sexual activity before marriage or even the rumors of such could have catastrophic impacts on a woman's economic livelihood. Some women would intentionally try to ruin another's reputation in order to elevate her own marrying potential. Language worked to reinforce this assumption that a "pure virgin" was much more valuable than a "dirty whore." In England prior to the settlers fleeing England, if a person broke the sexual rules, they were punished, and adhering to strict sexual norms left any behaviors falling outside of the box as deviant, sinful, and savage. Order was established by means of legality with, at times, harsh punishments for those that broke the established rules on gender and sexuality. This disconnection impacted sexuality in ways that we may not be fully able to understand. At minimum, offenders were shamed, and oftentimes publicly. Consequences could include lashings, whippings, flogging, branding, public stockings, mutilation, and execution (even burned at the stake). Lucie Fielding in her book *Trans Sex: Clinical Approaches to Trans Sexualities and Erotic Embodiments* writes,

> How we have sex, how we use our bodies to have sex, and what we consider sex to be in the first place, are all subject to regulation, surveillance, and input from the societies and cultures in which we have sex and experience our sexualities.
>
> (Fielding, 2021, p. 6)

This "regulation" and "surveillance" grew stronger and was maintained through violent punishments. This was a glimpse into the historical sexual trauma that the English brought with them to the colonies. I discuss historical sexual trauma in more detail in Chapter 5.

For now, I would like to take some time to think about patriarchy in the context of gender. As Gustafson was discussing in his TedTalk and as Iantaffi writes, "Our current understanding of gender is deeply impacted by settler colonial practices" (Iantaffi p. 23). The settlers arrived with a clearly established hierarchical binary of male and female with males holding the power, strength, citizenship, finances, and land ownership. Iantaffi sums it up by saying, "The historical tight control of sexuality, especially for people assigned female at birth and for queer people, is also linked to this need for governance of bodies that is essential to the settler colonial project" (Iantaffi, 2021, p. 30). Kim Tallbear has spoken about how religion, state laws, academia, and research have kept most of us living, for some uncomfortably, within the norms of settler sex and gender. This may be a good time to remind you that the settler colonial project was a successful plan that is still working today. Iantaffi writes, "Part of Christianization and settler colonialism has been the erasure of gender expansive identities, roles, and expressions and experiences" (Iantaffi, 2021, p. 26). Linguicide has limited our understanding of gender by erasing language that may have been more expansive and inclusive of all of our unique gender traits. Instead, settler sexuality shrunk the diversity and expression of gender into tightly knit gender and sexual roles.

Not only were people who fell outside this christian binary of male/female considered a threat, but also any system that was either egalitarian, not

strictly and biologically binary based, or matriarchal was also a threat to these views on which the rest of the settler colonial project was being built.
(Iantaffi, 2021, p. 30)

With violence, punishment, and shame at its center, all of this history is the formation of the sociosexual scripts that we still adhere to today. I think of settler sexuality as this box of acceptable sexual norms and practices that originated in the Americas through colonization. I use that box as a lens to interpret the joys and sufferings in modern-day American human sexuality. It offers some understanding as to how "normal" sexuality was created and perpetuated in the USA. Patriarchy is at the core of settler sexuality. Iantaffi writes, "Whiteness can, in fact, not be separated from the need to control gender in rigid ways. We could also say that we cannot talk of gender without talking about how bodies are racialized" (Iantaffi, 2021, p. 31). Therefore, we will be exploring the intersection between race and sexuality, ethnosexuality in Chapter 2.

Reflection

Were you aware of some of these historical pieces of patriarchy that I shared? What would you add?
How do you think the disruption of power between genders impacts sexuality and ethnosexuality today?
How has hetero-cis-patriarchy impacted your family of origin?
How are you benefiting from the effects of patriarchy?
How do you see patriarchy impacting your life now?
Iantaffi discusses "decentering of cisgender male heterosexuality as the baseline within Western Scientific discourse" (Iantaffi, 2021). How can you decenter white, cis-hetero, western paradigms in your personal life and in your work?

Case

Mary, a 44-year-old cis, bi-sexual, African American woman is partnered with Charles, a 32-year-old cis-hetero-sexual old African American man. Mary and Charles have recently started attending swinging parties. Charles has been somewhat resistant to joining the swinging lifestyle. He agreed to participate as long as they only play (share in sexual activities) together and only with other women, never men. Mary recently told Charles that she would like to start playing with men. This devastated Charles and he regretted agreeing to opening up their relationship to women. They attempted to go to their local swingers' club, a predominantly white space, two times, since Mary asked to have men as an option to play with. The first time, Charles was withdrawn and chose not to engage with anyone sexually, so Mary joined in conversation with a large group. The second time they went out, Charles became heavily intoxicated, which they reported had never happened before. Charles said,

"I normally nurse one beer all night." While at the party, Mary was talking with a smaller group of friends, Charles grabbed her arm and said, "We are going outside NOW! We are leaving!" He proceeded to pull her by the arm until they were outside. Due to his intoxication, he failed to notice that the group of friends had followed them out of concern. Charles cornered Mary against a fence and started yelling, "You wanna fuck him? Huh? Is that what you want? You wanna fuck that muthafucka?" Mary was shocked and confused by who and what he was talking about. She quickly caught the gaze of her friends watching them and froze. Getting no response from her, Charles became louder, more agitated, and inched toward her. Two white men approached Charles hoping to deescalate him; however, Charles punched one of them, causing the other man to have a bloody nose. He began yelling "You wanna fuck my wife, don't you?" repeatedly while charging the men. A third white man snuck up behind Charles and put him in a sleeper hold, a wrestling move where a person wraps their arm around their opponent's neck and tightens their bicep until the person loses consciousness. When he recovered consciousness, two of their women friends gave them a ride home. Any time they have tried to discuss what happened that evening or going back to the club, they find themselves in conflict for several days. I had seen them for five sessions prior to this day, and I had assessed for domestic violence and alcohol and substance abuse during the intake. Both denied any abuse occurring in the relationship. This was their first therapy session after the conflict at the event.

Case

I like to offer my clients the opportunity to guide the session into areas where they want to focus their healing. I find it helpful to request my client's permission to open emotionally sensitive conversations. I want them to have some anatomy in the room that they may not receive from the outside world when therapy ends.

Therapist: It sounds like you all have really been through it since I saw you last.
Charles: We sure have.
Therapist: Do you think it would be helpful for us to process what's going on for the both of you?
Mary: Yeah.
Charles: That's why we are paying you.
Therapist: Okay. Thank you for allowing the space for us all to process this together. I'm wondering, if you both have a hypothesis as to why you're struggling right now?

I'm using "us all" to emphasize that I am in relationship with them, and we are here together with intention. These clients had trouble navigating this discussion on their own. When I received permission, I demonstrated appreciation for them opening the space to discuss this with me.

Charles: You know it started going south when she started to wanna fuck other people.

Therapist: Mary, would you agree that's when the problems started?

Mary: I can understand why he is saying that. Because, I think that is when the problems started for him. I don't think it was a specific time that it started but more like a theme. (She hesitates before continuing). I think he always has to have control.

Charles: (throws his hands in the air) Why do you keep saying that?! She always says that!

Mary: (looks at the therapist) And . . . he continues to make decisions without me?

Charles: What do you mean? I never make any decisions without you.

Mary: You grabbed my body and said, "We are leaving!"

Charles: I know that because you keep telling me that but I don't remember what happened after I left the bar with my drink. (He turns to the therapist) I was very drunk that night.

Therapist: Like black out drunk.

Charles: Yea.

Mary: That's what he says, but that seems so convenient.

Charles: Bottom line, I don't control anything. You do what you want with the house. You go to work. What am I controlling?

Therapist: Do you mind if I interrupt here?

They both nod yes.

Therapist: I was wondering if we could explore what both of you are saying. Charles, your hypothesis was the relationship took a turn once y'all opened up. Mary, your hypothesis is that control is the underbelly of this conflict. Do I have that right?

I pause until both signals yes.

Charles: Sure, she thinks that I run everything. But, I don't.

Therapist: I think that sometimes we get into conflict because we feel like we are not being heard. My hypothesis is that neither one of you is feeling heard right now. Would you both agree with that?

I felt it was important, as a member of the relationship that the three of us in the room share, so I also include my hypothesis and allow the clients to respond.

Charles: Yea.

Mary looks away.

Therapist: Mary?
Mary: Yes. (A tear comes down her face.)
Therapist: Sometimes when we aren't being heard we can get frustrated, confused, and hurt. Being heard and seen can be some strong medicine. But, coming from a place where we are fighting to be heard, we have a difficult time listening. We've talked a little bit about the brain and body connection and what happens when we become activated. So, we know the importance of soothing ourselves and at times practicing co-regulation. Can we take a minute to collectively ground now?

   Both nod their heads.
   I am slowing down the session to model for the clients that we do not need to act in urgency to get our points across. Through slowing down we can regulate and soothe activation that surfaces around this conflict. Slowing down the session to regulate is also modeling how clients can practice the skill of slowing down when in discussions outside of therapy.

Therapist: Ok, so you both have taken breaths with me before. I want to take a few breaths together like we normally do, then, I'm going to switch it up a little bit. Is that cool?

They both nod.

Therapist: Ok, cool. Thank you for trusting me on this. Now, let's take those 3 breaths together. In through the nose for a count of four and out through the mouth for a count of 6. I actually like to be audible with my exhale to allow the vibrations to reach more places than my breath can. I welcome you to do the same. I will mute myself on the exhale, as not to distract you. You are welcome to let out even the slightest sounds. Feel free to close your eyes or keep them open. Ok, now, let's start the three breaths with the last breath being the biggest one you have taken all day.

   All three of us take three synchronized breaths. On the third breath they both released an audible sigh.

Therapist: Good, now I want you to continue breathing slowly and deeply. I want you to turn your attention to the sensations in your body. Let's take some time to notice any activation that is sitting in our body and listen to any messages it has for us.

This couple received psychoeducation on the importance of regulation of the nervous system, especially in moments of conflict. This is their first prompt for listening to their body in session.

Therapist: Okay, can both of you take turns sharing if and where you have any activation in your body?

Charles: What do you mean?

Therapist: Let's scan our body and pay attention to any sensations that we feel. Any tightness, warmth, tingle, or sting.

Mary: I'm feeling heaviness around my eyes.

Therapist: Good noticing, Mary.

Mary: It feels like a gallon of tears is behind them but the tears are blocked from coming out. (one lone tear slowly falls down her check)

Therapist: Thank you for sharing, Mary. If you are comfortable, I want you to sit with this discomfort of this pressure behind your eyes. Know that you are welcome to breathe into the pressure or to release some of the pressure with your tears. (She begins to bite her lip). Charles, is it okay to make some time to sit with this pressure. (He offers a reluctant and fearful nod).

Charles: I got you babe. You know I got you. (He puts his hand on her knee in an attempt to reassure her).

Therapist: How does Charles' hand feel on your knee? Would you like it there? Or would you like him to move it? (Mary grabbed his hand and hugged it into her chest. She let out a wail and one tear fell down the other cheek).

Mary: I'm tired. I'm sad. I'm too tired to fight.

Therapist: I hear you. This has been troubling you both for some time now. Today, we are going to do some hard work, however, we are not going to fight. Okay? (She nods). You both are already doing this now, but I would really like to set our intentions for listening and speaking from a place of care and kindness rather than defensiveness and attack or withdrawal. It feels to me that there are many stories and feelings attached to this. As we proceed, it's going to be helpful if you can be mindful of absolutes. There is always an exception to an "always" or "never." Also, pay attention to when criticism and defensiveness start to come out of you.

Therapist: (looks at Charles) What sensations do you have in your body now?

Charles: Well, I am a little uptight. Like I don't know what is going on.

Therapist: Where do you feel that in your body?

Charles: Well, my chest is tight. My legs feel like they want to run.

Therapist: Good noticing. Can we sit with those sensations?

Charles: Yes.

Therapist: Both of you have done some nice work in noticing what is happening in your bodies. You both have some strong feelings inside, like sadness and fear, that others can't see. It appears that in this conflict, you have not shared some of these deeper, more hidden emotions and sensations with each other.

Mary: It's true. We haven't.

Therapist: Sometimes these sensations that we feel in our body are trying to send us messages or protect us in some way. I want you to picture those sensations you described to us. Can you feel them or see them in your imagination? (Both nod). Okay, can you give them a name?

Mary: Ha, if I had to give mine a name it would be sadness or weepy.

Therapist: hmm, how about the Weeping Sadness?

Mary: (she smiles) yea, that'll work.

Charles: I've got real Pop vibes.

Therapist: What do you mean? (Mary laughs)

Charles: We used to joke that my dad always had his running shoes on. He would get really angry and never showed it. After his first heart attack, the doctors told him to decrease stress and get more exercise. After that, whenever he would get upset, he would just walk out the door and kept walking until he could calm down. When things got heated, you'd see him go for his shoes. Nobody tried to stop him because everybody was worried, he would have another heart attack. I feel like my feet are calling for my running shoes.

Therapist: I see. How about we call this part Lil Pop Vibes?

Charles: (laughs) yea. That's good.

Therapist: I don't know if this sounds right to you, but I was thinking both pops and Little Pops didn't really feel like they could express their true feelings sometimes. I say this mainly because men are socialized to have very limited acceptable expressions of emotion. Anger is one of them. Maybe those running shoes are avoiding other feelings as well.

This is a reminder that patriarchy hurts everyone—even cis-het men. This is an example of reminding the client of the pressures of limiting emotional expressions to what are deemed acceptable for men.

Therapist: As we move forward. I want you to remember that these parts of us are always with us and have a tendency to override us with extreme emotion. What do you think Weeping Sadness and Lil Pop Vibes are trying to tell you with the tightness in your legs, feeling that you want to run, or the pressure of tears behind the eye?

Mary:	Like I said, I know I'm sad and tired. Maybe something is stopping me from getting all these tears out.
Charles:	Hmm . . . I'm sorry you're sad. To be completely honest, I'm scared. I don't want to lose her. Maybe I want to run away from that feeling. I wanna fix it but I feel like I'm failing.
Therapist:	Know the Lil Pop Vibes and Weeping Sadness or other parts of yourself may make an appearance. It's okay to invite them in and ask them what they have to say or want to contribute.
Charles:	I'm actually feeling bad about calling that part Lil Pop Vibes.
Therapist:	Oh yea?
Charles:	Yea, my pops was a solid man.
Therapist:	Yea?
Charles:	He was faithful. He was the pastor of our church. He worked a lot to support my mother and all of us kids. He handled everything! I know that I could never live up to him. In fact, I haven't been ready to propose to Mary because I don't even have my life together like that.
Mary:	I didn't know that babe (she whispers with another single tear falling to her chin).
Charles:	I didn't even want to get married until I knew I could provide for us. I struggle every day to make sure we have a little bit of savings in the bank.
Therapist:	That sounds heavy, Charles.
Charles:	I'm terrified to have children because I do not feel like I can be half the father and provider that my father was. We don't even have a church to raise our children in. (his voice cracks when he talks) It is. It is heavy. And now . . . we have sex with other people.
Therapist:	Trying to measure up to a strong patriarch that is religious, monogamous, and financially able is a lot of pressure. I truly believe that patriarchy does not just harm women, but it is an incredible disservice to us all and this is an example of this. The pressure of being a patriarch or "man of the house" are unreal.

(Charles locks eyes with the therapist)

Charles:	Nobody has ever said it like that to me and it's so true!
Therapist:	We have these ideas of what it means to be a man, partner, father. Or, what our relationships are "supposed" to look like and our roles in them. And, sometimes what we are doing is perpetuating the patriarchy. And, that hurts everyone.
Mary:	I always thought about patriarchy like with gender roles.
Therapist:	Oh, yes of course. Historically, patriarchy has had a huge impact on gender roles. Have you two ever discussed gendered roles in this relationship?

Mary: A little bit. I know that he wants me to do more housework than him, that's a gender role, right? (She does not wait for a response from either of us before continuing) I think he would prefer I not work. It's good for him if I cook in the kitchen, but I can't touch the BBQ or the smoker, you see what I'm saying? (She tilts her head with a little grin).

Everyone smiles.

Therapist: I would like to bring in this helpful tool that helps us look at our positionality in the world and our relationships. It will give us the opportunity to explore monogamy, gender, religion, finances, power differentials, and more. Does this sound like it would be helpful for you?

Charles: I think so.

Mary: Yes!

Therapist: Ok, it's called the Expanded Addressing Model, have you heard of it? (They both shake their head "no"). It was originally developed by Pamela Hays, but I'm been kinda taking my own spin on it. Do you mind going through it with me? (The therapist shares a screen to show the Expanded Addressing Model PDF and explains the mode). We will go through each of these domains at some point and process our positions within each. You probably will not be able to complete it during this session, so your homework this week will be to finish where we left off and bring your discussion back to me next week. Cool?

Charles: Sounds good.

Mary: Yes, it does.

Therapist: There are a few domains I would like to get to in session today, then y'all can circle back and review the ones we don't get to in session today.

Out of the 17 domains, I decided to focus on the (A) Age and generational influences, (R) Religion and Relationship status, (S) Socioeconomic Status (Class) and Sexual orientation, (G) Gender. When working the Addressing Model in session, we talked in more depth about Charles' insecurities around being younger than Mary. We discussed how being younger made him feel in a lower position of power and explored the feelings associated with his expectations of manhood. We shared in a discussion around insecurities that made him want to compensate for the age gap by being the "breadwinner." He was making less money and carried incredible amounts of shame because of it. We also explored how ageism could be impacting the power dynamics in the therapy room, with Mary and myself being similar in age. They both expressed differences in how they identify their sexual orientation and religion.

In looking at religion, Charles felt that christianity was the right way to be "a man" and that to be a good father, you brought your children to church. Mary's beliefs sounded more agnostic, although she did not identify as such. I was able to highlight the pressure from being younger, feeling this need to provide, and to be a man of god. I acknowledged that having a partner with a different sexual and relationship orientation challenges some of his belief on what it is to be a man. We discussed gender and how Mary experiences sexism in their relationship. I also took a moment to discuss how men are typically socialized to think anger and aggression are okay emotions to have, yet being vulnerable with other emotions such as sadness or fear can emasculate. We dropped back into the memory of the conflict at the party and addressed the conflict looking through the lens of gender. They identified that the men expressed more anger and physical aggression, while the women nurtured and cared for them. I asked the couple if they felt race had played a part in this conflict. Mary said, "How could it not. We are basically the only Black people ever there. Now, he's the Black dude that lost his shit at the club which wasn't too flattering. He's basically surrounded by white dudes and 'taken down.'" We then began to explore what feelings come up for both of them having this happen in a white space and to be taken down by white men. I asked Charles if race had anything to do with his insecurities the night of the event. He said, "Nah, well maybe. Sexually, I'm not insecure, but those white guys have a lot more money than me."

Charles drew a connection of his age creating insecurity and causing him to want to compensate in other ways. When he could not do that financially, his insecurities increased. He reported feeling envious of the men at the party because they drove "fancy cars," took luxurious trips, and some of them made enough money that their wives did not have to work. He felt less of a man in comparison because he could not "provide" in that way. After processing further, he said, "I just can't keep up." He felt pressure to show up in this space with what sounded to me like relatively wealthy people, so he hid his feelings of inadequacy. He felt pressure from the people at the party because he felt like they were expecting him to be performative as the only Black man in the space. We were able to name the fetishism he often experiences in these spaces. He valued monogamy and had negative internalized messages around what it meant for his woman to be penetrated by someone else. He expressed fear of being in an open relationship due to his christian beliefs and of losing Mary, if they opened up the relationship. He said, "this is why I'm holding on so tight." After further discussion of what it looks like to "hold on so tight," he said, "Ahhh, babe (looking at Mary)! This is that control piece you've been trying to tell me about." (He looks at the therapist.) So is this me (he puts up an air quote gesture and mimics the therapists voice "perpetuating the patriarchy"?)

The therapist smiles. Mary smiles and both of her eyes fill with tears, and they drop quickly three at a time down her face.

2   Sango

Sango is the orisha of lightning and thunder. He is one of the strongest mighty warriors.

Colorism-privileging the proximity to whiteness based on the color of one's skin.

Texturism-Texturism can be thought of as favoring straight hair, while curly and kinky hair is seen as unattractive, unprofessional or unruly.

Featurism-A preference for eurocentric standards of beauty within facial features.

It is my hope that you have a general understanding that white cis-hetero-patriarchy has permeated most of the systems we are a part of. We are moving forward in this chapter to examine the intersection between ethnicity/race and sexuality. Before you start, below I have offered some questions to reflect on. I encourage you to journal your answers.

Reflection

Did you ever feel you were more or less attractive due to the color of your skin?

Did you ever feel you were more or less attractive due to the texture or color of your hair?

Did you ever feel you were more or less attractive due to the size or shape of your body?

Have you ever felt more or less attractive due to the size, shape, or color of your genitalia?

Have you ever felt safe or unsafe in a clinical setting due to your ethnicity/race, gender, sexual orientation, and partner choices?

What are sexualized stereotypes, beliefs, and thoughts you have been exposed to about people from your same racial groups?

What are sexualized stereotypes, beliefs, and thoughts you have been exposed to about people from different racial groups?

Have you fetishized people from another race? Has someone fetishized you?

DOI: 10.4324/9781003276951-3

I hope you were able to take some time to reflect on these questions. If you are experiencing any unsettling now, please take a moment to give yourself something you may need. Maybe it's a simple as a breath, stretch, a glass of water, or a call or text to a friend. Maybe you want to consider processing any unsettling with your own therapist or a loved one. I have some practice in sitting in the discomfort that arises when looking at our harmful history and how it has impacted my own thoughts of race and sexuality (DiAngelo, 2012). A few years back, my academic work took a turn and started simmering at the intersection of race/ethnicity and sexuality. "Ethnosexuality" is a term coined by Joane Nagel (2000) to describe that intersection. In *Ethnicity and Sexuality* Nagel writes, "No ethnic boundary is more sexualized, surveilled, and scrutinized in US society than the color line dividing blacks and whites" (p. 122). When looking at ethnosexuality, I feel it necessary to discuss white body supremacy and how it continues to harm Black sexualities. How ethnosexuality intersects for a white woman, looks much different than the same intersection does for Black women. The works of Resmaa Menekeem, Robin DiAngelo, and Layla Said will be used to solidify the understanding of white-dominant discourse and its effects. Miscegenation, the prevention of races coming together in intimate ways, will also be discussed in this chapter. Nagel (2002) wrote that we need to

> expose the sexualized foundations of ethnicity by examining the ways in which the rule breaking, policing, and punishment of sexual deviants serves both to challenge and to reinforce racial, ethnic, and nationalist boundaries and hegemonies and to strengthen ethnosexual regimes.
>
> (p. 118)

A greater understanding of American miscegenation offers us insight into American ethnosexuality through interracial sexual violence.

I believe a foundational piece of ethnosexuality is white supremacy. I focus on white body supremacy and how it continues to be projected onto Black sexualities. Now, I feel like most of us know what white supremacy is and its impacts. Before the racial uprisings in 2020, when I presented on colonization and sex, I had a similar experience to what Menekeem writes about. Many of the attendees connected the term "white" supremacy with fundamentalists, Nazis, or the Klu Klux Klan. However, what seems more easily understood just a few years later is that white supremacy isn't just some group of people fighting for the purity of the white race. In the book *What Does it Mean to Be White?*, Robin DiAngelo writes,

> White supremacy does not refer to individual white people per se and their individual intentions, but to a political economic social system of domination. This system is based on the historical and current accumulation of structural power that privileges, centralizes, and elevates white people as a group.
>
> (DiAngelo, 2012)

With white supremacy comes white superiority. DiAngelo writes, "White superiority stems directly from white supremacy's belief that people with white or white passing skin are better than and therefore deserve to dominate over people with brown or black skin" (DiAngelo, 2012). White supremacy does not only exist in the lucid and cognitive mind. It is something that is embedded into our bodies, systems, and structures so much so that we are not always privy to them. Resmaa Menekeem, author of *My Grandmother's Hands: Racialized Trauma and the Pathway to Mending Our Hearts and Bodies*, explains how white supremacy became interwoven into existence and maintained. He writes, "It is part of the operating system and organizing structure of American culture. It's always functioning in the background, often invisibly, in our institutions, our relationships, and our interactions" (Menakem, 2017). As a sexologist, it is the sexual interactions that I want us to pay attention to, while including a historical sexual context, to bring more insight to the traumas that are insidiously embedded in our bodies and communities. David Archer author of *Anti-Racist Psychotherapy: Confronting systemic racism and healing racial trauma*, tells us, "White fragility is a trauma-driven process that is embedded deep in the nervous system. The dissociation of topics of race in our society is as deeply embedded as our dissociation from our bodies" (Archer, 163). Part of our job as sexuality professionals is to invite our clients back into their bodies. To decrease dissociation and live in the present with decreased distress. How do we do this when a presenting problem is embedded in white supremacy? Tracie Gilbert's in her book *Black and Sexy: A Framework of Racialized Sexuality* writes, "The average sexuality of an African American—or maybe even black person's diasporically—cannot be fully understood without attending to the specific treatment of racial isolation provided by white supremacy and anti-blackness" (Gilbert, 2022, p. 2). Tending to white supremacy and anti-Blackness is imperative for doing this work. Understanding historical trends is practically necessary to make that happen. The racialized sexual isolation of Black people during colonial days is hardly discussed. For the settlers, "proper" sexuality came after marriage; however, enslaved people did not have marrying rights. At times, they were forced into unions that were arranged by their owners. There are documents of enslaved people reporting, in detail, how their masters would punish them if they did not have sex for procreation. Resentments grew between these couples as they were forced, at times by gunpoint, to have sex with their arranged partner. Please consider that the transatlantic slave trade was abolished in 1808, and it was not until 1866 with the formation of the 13th Amendment that Black folx were able to legally marry and own property. When newly freed people in quasimarriages, or marriages arranged by their enslavers, were freed, they were looked down upon or punished for leaving their arranged relationship. Many longed for and searched for their chosen partners. Single newly freed people were also pressured to enter marriage and christianity. Amatonormativity's influence pressured freed Black folx to marry the opposite sex and maintain a cis-het-couple centric household.

When it comes to crossing the racialized boundary of Black and white, strong evidence of how anti-Blackness and white supremacy entered sexuality and intimacy can be seen in the anti-miscegenation laws. Let us not forget that anti-miscegenation, the prevention of races coming together in intimate ways, was upheld in our very recent past, 1967 to be exact. In the case of *Loving v. Virginia*, the Supreme Court unanimously overturned the 1924 Racial Integrity Act. While some worked to keep the races from mixing, others delighted in interracial sexual unions. In 1625, Thomas Morton started a plantation in Plymouth, where he invited Indigenous locals to have sex with him and other settlers in Merry Mount. This appalled other settlers who were there to "create godly communities built on the centrality of the family." He was deported and imprisoned in such horrific conditions that he died shortly after his release (D'Emilio & Freedman, 2012). In the United States, we start to see the criminalization of interracial relationships around the 1660s (Solomon, 2017).

Early on when the European settlers first arrived, they did not enforce laws around interracial relationships. D'Emilio and Freedman explain,

Only after slavery became entrenched during the late seventeenth century did southern legislatures ban marriage between blacks and whites. Illicit unions persisted, however, mulattoes accounted for over one-fifth of the children born out of wedlock in Virginia at the turn of the century.

(D'Emilio & Freedman, 2012, p. 14)

This meant that although laws were in place to prevent sexual and relational boundary crossing, we have tangible evidence that white men were raping and impregnating enslaved African American women after such laws were established. This should cause one to consider that these laws were in place to protect white women, rather than all people, especially not Black folx. "White men could rape female slaves without fear of punishment" (Treatment of Slaves in the United States, 2022). While Black men were being severely punished with castration or even death for sexual activity with white people, this system seemed to protect white men from the same consequences. Since a Black enslaved woman had no legal rights, she was unable to report sexual assault as her white counterparts could. However, a master could take legal action against someone who damaged their human property. Solomon points out that "Slaves had separate criminal courts and juries, lower standards of evidence, guilty until proven innocent burdens of proof, and harsher sentencing" (Solomon, 2017). The majority of the Black men who were tried for sexual assault were sentenced to death—in comparison to the only 10 percent of white men being sentenced to death for the same crime. These disparities between white men and Black men's sentencing that we saw in the colonial past are echoing even to the present day.

One of the most blatant indicator of the sexual assault and rape of Black AFAB perpetrated by AMAB (assigned female at birth/assigned male at birth) people was the generation of what was called "mulatto" children, that is, mixed-race children that were born during the time. As I alluded to before, English common law was that children were granted the status of their father. Servitude was handed down matrilineally. There is evidence of some patriarchs freeing their mixed-race children; however, the majority did not grant them freedom. Since their children were born into slavery, these fathers did not have the responsibility to support them, like they did their white children. Visitors to the south witnessed the growing number of men "taking sexual advantage of slave women" when they saw for themselves the number of mix-raced children that inhabited the area. "The 1850 census identified 245,000 slaves as mulatto; by 1860, there were 411,000 slaves classified as mulatto out of a total slave population of 3,900,000" (Treatment of Slaves in the United States, 2022). For reference, slavery was abolished in 1865.

This blending of racialized borders added another dimension to colorism. I define colorism as privileging the proximity to whiteness based on the color of one's skin. I mentioned earlier that most of the colonizers categorized folx on a racial hierarchy with white being favored and determining status. It was backed by scientists and researchers. Carl Linnaeus developed a race classification system utilizing color (Degruy, 2017, p. 42). This reinforced a discrimination against or privilege for someone's skin tone. Colorism is so closely intertwined with texturism and featurism. Texturism is favoring straight hair deeming it appealing, while curly and kinky hair is seen as unattractive, unprofessional, or unruly. Featurism is a preference for eurocentric standards of beauty within facial features. I believe body type and shape may also be considered. Colorism, texturism, featurism, and euro standards of beauty brought an erotic under tone to bi- or multiracial people. Their possible lighter skin, euro features, combined with the assimilation of "American" culture as a second- or third-generation African played in to the eroticizing of theses light-skinned people with no legal rights. As enslaved people, they too were not legally protected from the sexual harm their mother's endured to create them. Erotizing and fetishizing light-skinned people will be discussed further in Chapter 3. It's important to remember that colorism, texturism, featurism, and fatphobia are all holdovers from our past that is very vibrant in modern days. These are measures still used today to determine desirability, acceptability, and "pretty privilege."

Moving forward through time to present-day interracial relationships, we have made social, political, and relational strides in how our society views them. However, an important point to consider is that in 1968, 73 percent of US citizens disapproved of the right to marry interracially. This dropped to 17 percent by 2007. This questioned asked whether one agreed to the idea of interracial relationships and did not account for whether the person themself would actually date outside of their race. Interestingly what I found was that "less than 46% of white Americans are willing to date an individual of any other race" (Race & Sexuality, 2022). I wish they could have added the question, "are you willing to have sex with an individual of any other race." Needless to say, there are still people that do not think races should cross an intimacy boundary and even more people that would not choose to be in an interracial relationship themselves. Livingston and Brown reported that only about 4 percent of white folx in the United States will marry outside of their race. That means that overall, white people will generally date someone outside of their race but will only rarely commit to marriage with a person outside of their race. Using marriage as a way of measuring a legitimate partnership is, of course, problematic. As many of us know, there are many partnerships that are not accounted for when we only include marriage as a defining measure of love and commitment. Nonetheless, examining marriage is, at this time, a measurable variable that cannot be disregarded in terms of how white people really feel about interracial relationships. This racial discrimination can also be measured in the online dating platform on in the media.

Media has a profound interpretation of ethnosexuality that unfortunately comes from a very racist, cis-hetero-normative, ablest, and transphobic lens. When someone's personal sexual bias is shared with the dominant culture, it becomes a part of the system of oppression against the marginalized group. The media's influence on how sexualities of marginalized groups are portrayed and perceived perpetuate harm, including sexual assaults against said groups. Tropes of Black women become solidified through media, television, and movies. You may have heard of Some: Jezebel, Mammy, and Sapphire. Jezebel is a hypersexualized insatiable caricature that is beautiful and ready for sex. Mammy is portrayed as almost this asexual caregiver, while Sapphire is an emasculating angry Black woman. Later, during the Reagan administration, the Welfare Queen is born. She left the impression that Black women would intentionally have more babies in order to receive more government assistance. All tropes come with a sexual narrative that slowly weaved itself into popular culture. When I teach human sexuality or sex therapy-related courses, I ask my students to look at the historical, political, and legal background of a topic in discussion. I also ask my students to consider how the topic or people are being represented in the media, in our cultures, and in our homes.

Now, I would like you to take some time reflecting on the following questions.

Reflection

What are sexualized racial stereotypes you have seen of BILPOC folx in historic times or present day? What are sexualized racial stereotypes you have seen of white people?

How has white supremacy influenced your views on sexuality?

Have you heard your family say any racialized sexual stereotypes?

What racist beliefs have you internalized from your race, family, culture, etc.?

In what ways have you seen white sexuality centered in print and film?

How has our culture sexualized some BILPOC while desexualizing other parts?

As a child, did you find representations of your race in media? If so, how was their sexuality portrayed?

How do you see colorism playing into modern-day sexuality?

What sexualized racialized descriptive messages have you been exposed to?

How have you seen BILPOCC sexuality neglected or minimized?

How have you discounted or ignored BILPOCC sexualities?

Have you ever felt entitlement over another body? Has it felt like someone was entitled to your body?

Have you fetishized another body? Has another body fetishized you?

What have you begun to understand about your personal experiences with sexuality in relation to white supremacy?

In what ways have you stayed silent or complicit to sexualized stereotypes?

What are some ways you can begin to have deeper conversations with your community around ethnosexuality?

How does white privilege show up in your professional field?

How can your professional field decenter whiteness?

3 Ibeji

Ibeji are twin embodying one orisha.

The history lessons I received from my youth all the way up to my post-graduate studies in sexuality have failed me in fully understanding the sexual commodification of slavery. In order to move forward in liberation, I believe it is important to look back with critical analysis to examine our harmful past. It is our past that has grounded us in a present-shared reality that is harming so many. As a sexologist, I believe it is imperative that we look at American history centering sexuality. Emphasis on sexology in this historical context can assist us in creating anti-colonial practices within our field now.

Before we proceed further in this chapter, I would like you to take some time to journal about the following questions:

Reflection

What do you remember about what you were taught about slavery during early education?

How was slavery discussed throughout the rest of your academic journey? How about in your sexuality studies?

What have you learned about the sexual commodification of enslaved peoples in the United States?

Why do you think the full truth about some historical events has not been told?

What do you see when you envision an enslaver? How do you see their age, gender, and race in your imagination?

What is your perception of white women's role in slavery?

The American common knowledge of history that was taught in public education, especially around sex and race, has been censored and romanticized. Many of us grew up thinking what we were taught was the true history. Don't get me wrong, not all of what we were taught is incorrect or false. However, many times, our history lessons were taught through a pair of rose-colored glasses that went over our collective eyes. Preventing us from seeing all the truth for what it was—ugly, inhumane, traumatizing, brutal, and evil. The

DOI: 10.4324/9781003276951-4

following is a part of American sex history that all too often gets left out of academia and sexuality discourse.

Originally, Africans that were brought to America were indentured servants. This meant that they worked for seven to ten years before being freed (Baptist, 2014). With capitalization fueling the transatlantic slave trade, those that were profiting from the labor of Africans quickly realized how much more money they would make if they could own another human for the entirety of their life. With this realization, laws came to be passed that made the process of freeing Black people more challenging and penalized them with harsher punishments for an attempt of escape. Africans became the largest minority group, quickly outnumbering the Indigenous population. Although laws were in place prohibiting sexual contact between races, as I mentioned before, these miscegenation laws were in place to protect white people. Solomon writes, "rape and sexual violence became another way for whites to reify dominance and control over blacks." Women's sexuality of the colonial era was split into a binary. White women were seen as sexually pure, and BILPOC woman were not. Nkiru Nzegwu, author of the chapter *"Osunality" (or African eroticism)* articulates how this harmful assumption was perpetuated. "Imperialism racialised sexuality world-wide, and colonialism, apartheid a corporate globalization reconstituted only white women into paragons of purity and beauty and deserving of love and affection, and fetishized non-white bodies as expendable and worthless" (Nzegwu, 2011, p. 255). Comparing the enthonosexualities' of Black women and white women in the colonial days highlights the contrast of that time. There is noticeable incongruence in women's sexuality that is extremely visible. Black women were portrayed as Nzegwu puts it, "more sexual, less moral, less beautiful, less delicate" and "such claims allegedly excused rape, the rejection of children, the sale of lovers, and the practice of forcing black women to labor in jobs for which white women were ostensibly too delicate" (Nzegwu, 2011). One of the most profound quotes I have heard about sexuality during slavery came from the book *The Half Has Never Been Told: Slavery and the Making of American Capitalism*, Edward Baptist tells us, "Slavery's frontier was a white man's sexual playground" (Baptist, 2014, p. 238). All of the forbidden desires denied in solitude or within settler marriage were being quenched by enslaved people. This chapter examines some historical sexual traumas of children and adults of all genders, highlighting not only the sadistic past of individuals but also the system that created the culture of abuse.

Pause

I attended a webinar with Resmaa Menekeem called *Somatic Medicine and COVID-19: Webinar for Healers of Color*. It was June 2020, just a few months after the killing of Breonna Taylor and just one month after the killing of George Floyd. Community uprisings spread almost as fast as the global pandemic. At the time, the outside world seemed like such a scary place, being held and seen in that space full of healers that too were wounded by the social climate was comforting. All of us trying to navigate the uncertain terrain of our lives and therapeutic shifts and strains in our work, we all looked tired, yet relieved, we found a place to rest and heal ourselves. After the training, I decided to continue with Somatic Abolitionism and Cultural Somatics and joined a nine-month communal space with the Education for Racial Equity led by Resmaa and Erin Trent Johnson. Each month we spent a couple of hours with the two of them learning content and skills. We also met once a month with our triads, three people from the larger group that you shared the nine-month journey with, to practice the skills. We also collectively read *My Grandmother's Hands*. There are few things I want to share with you that I learned from brother Resmaa and this work. First, one is to pause. That's it. Sounds simple right? Not exactly. I witnessed Resmaa do many live demos. He stayed in-tune with the participant and took notice of when disorientating emotions arise or activation occurs. When he sensed it, he said one word, "pause." With this one word, he is inviting you to slow down, to feel with the body and not with the words. Resmaa encouraged us to "use the VIMBAS": (V)ibes and vibrations, (I)mages and thoughts, (M)eaning making, (B)ehaviors and urges, (A)ffect and feeling, (S)ensations. We all had journals where we would "scribe" not use our intellectual and cognitive brain to write, but to allow our bodies to take the pen and scribe from another place of knowing. Sometimes we need to slow down in order to process the information before us. Our bodies need to metabolize and settle. If you feel yourself reacting from urgency, needing to complete the section quickly, or skipping it outright, ask yourself why and invite yourself to slow down. Think about Resmaa's VIMBAS and take a moment to examine what's going on inside.

Resmaa writes,

> Trauma is all about speed and reflexivity—which is why, in addressing trauma, each of us needs to work through it slowly, over time. We need to understand our body's process of connection and settling. We need to slow ourselves down and learn to lean into uncertainty, rather than away from it. We need to ground ourselves, touch the pain or discomfort inside of trauma, and explore it—gently. This requires building a tolerance for bodily and emotional discomfort, and learning to stay present with—rather than trying to flee—that discomfort.
>
> (Menakem, 2017, p. 14)

You don't have to read every word, but I encourage you to use introspection on which pieces you distance yourself from or when you start to notice any sensations or dissociation. When pausing, you're welcome to break out your own journal or paper and pen and "scribe" what your body, your inner knower, your ancestors, or other influences have to say. Many times, when Resmaa told someone to pause, you could tell they did not want to. They wanted to keep on going by expressing themselves verbally. Resmaa would repeat, "Pause." When the participant paused and had to sit with the feeling, you could see a well of emotion come over them. Many times, tears were present, anger could be seen burning through their face, or an incredible sadness encapsulates them. When that happened, he would say, "I got you" then later add, "we got you." He would encourage us to look at each other holding space. Some nodded in solidarity, others held a hand on their hearts, some rocked their bodies back and forth, others used the Zoom heart reaction, all holding each other in communal pain, metabolizing trauma, learning, and healing. Energetically, you are not alone. I know you can't see me now but know that I am here with you. Holding you in uncomfortable spaces of what you may read.

Part of our work is, of course, grounding our bodies. I invite you to utilize whatever practice works for you. I discovered the importance of movement for my body when working with racialized historical and present-day trauma. Allowing my body to sway back and forth, bounce my knees up and down while standing, bouncing on my sit bones while sitting, roll my hips in a circular motion, stretching my shoulders and face muscles, assisted me in getting through the process of researching, teaching, and writing on the topic of colonization. One of my favorite and easiest interventions that Resmaa taught us was to look behind each shoulder, look above us, look at all the doors in the room, and look at any windows. This slows and orientates us back into the room. It also can provide safety knowing that there is no unknown danger lurking behind you. Racialized, sexualized, and historical trauma can make you feel like there is sometimes. Looking at the doors and windows is a reminder that you are not locked in a space. You are free to leave. Later, I will again invite you to take a pause. I encourage you to use that space to ground, rest, and process, as we continue looking at American sexual history.

We know that christianization was hand in hand with colonization. Some colonist stayed motivated by their religious convictions and adhered to a sexually strict moral code. Others were quenching their desires of lust and money with the sin of sexual exploitation. Baptist writes, "Many southwestern whites wanted proper forms of sexual morality to govern the public culture of the region. But that plan collapsed. The explosive growth of the interstate slave trade relentlessly forced the commodification of enslaved women's sexuality into view" (Baptist, 2014, p. 238). The people that stood on the side of morality, worked to maintain their sexual order by pointing out how slavery was impacting sexual mores of the colony. Baptist continues, "abolitionist critique focused on the way slavery disrupted family relationships and forced enslaved women into nonmarital sex" (Baptist, 2014, p. 240). Thus, reinforcing the sexualized nature involved with the sale of people. Abolitionist were fighting against the shared narratives within the colonial communities that fostered rape and abuse. Sometimes, it became even more nuanced. Some christian abolitionists may have used morality as a guise to hide their hatred toward the sexualized trade and have been motivated by alternative reasons to work to dismantle slavery. There are many accounts of white women forbidding or turning a blind eye to their husbands' affairs with enslaved women. Some women would intentionally sell off women that she felt were in competition. "These white women did not sell enslaved people out of necessity; they got rid of them because of shame, jealousy, and anger" (Jones-Rogers, 2019, p. 37).

Pause. Three breaths. Each one deeper than the last

Remember, Black women, as enslaved people, had no legal protection. They could not report an assault. White women could. White men who raped Black women suffered no consequences unless the enslaved persons' master's proceeded legal sanctions against a perpetrator for damage to their human property. Sadly, there are many court accounts of master's pressing charges against individuals who had sexually assaulted the people they owned. When a white woman reported being raped by a Black man, that man will have harsher consequences (e.g., longer incarceration sentencing, castration, death) than their white counterpart. Foster points out, "Castration and other genital mutilations served as punishment in the hands of overseers and owners as well as in popular depictions of public enforcement of 'justice'" (Foster, 2018, p. 129). Black men's genitalia were subject to scrutiny and punishment. Through this time grew the phallocentric focus on the Black male body. This caused disgust in some but intrigue for many others. In *Sexuality and Slavery: Reclaiming Intimate Histories in the Americas*, Berry and Harris (2018) write, "Many Europeans believed that people of African descent had no norms around sexual practice and thus were available for slave owners to enact their own emotional and sexual fantasies in relationships with enslaved people" (Berry and Harris, 2018, p. 2). With the sexual repression of the settler sexual script, one lacking of passion, desire, pleasure, and exploration, many enslavers used enslaved people to satisfy unmet sexual desires.

Baptist (2014) writes:

> Slavery permitted unchecked dominance and promised unlimited fulfillment of unrestrained desire. That made the behavior of entrepreneurs particularly volatile, risky, profitable, and disastrous. Then, in the 1830s, as white people, especially men, tried to build southwestern empires out of credit and enslaved human beings, they sought out more and more risk. This behavior planted the seeds for a cycle of boom and bust that would shape the course of American history, and one cannot understand it without studying both careful calculation and passionate craving.
>
> (p. 234)

Baptist links sexual desire and risk-taking through examining behavioral economics outcomes and ties it into his conclusion that demonstrates America's heightened hypersexualized slave trade. He found that there are "hardwired connections" between sexual desire and risk-taking decisions about buying and selling of people. "When researchers expose men to images of attractive, presumably available women, their propensity to take financial risks increases dramatically" (Baptist, p. 235). He writes that men were prone to act "financially aggressive when their brains are 'primed' by imagery of supposedly sexually available women, their propensity to take financial risks increased dramatically" (Baptist, p. 235). As a marketing ploy, slave markets were able to take advantage of this concept of selling sex on the auction block. "Sale time was when the forced sexualization of enslaved women's bodies was more explicit" (Baptist, 2014, p. 99). Forced to strip, so their bodies could be prodded and gazed upon for the assessment of attractiveness, strength, health, and reproductive abilities. "For the female half of the enslaved people traded and moved, sexual assault and exploitation shaped price and experiences. Traders manipulated buyers' fancies to make sales" (Baptist, p. 242). This sexual violence continued upon the sale of the enslaved person. "This energy magnified in 1819 when the 'legal right to rape one's human property would shape not only purchases of slaves but the broader behavior of entrepreneurs'" (Baptist, p. 181). Having this illicit underlying sexual drive with no legal ramifications meant that "purchase promised reward" (Baptist, 2014)—sexual reward. For many, the auction block was not the beginning of abuse. Some were assaulted on their native land by their captors, sexually abused during transport, or while in holding prior to purchase. It was not just master's that were the perpetrators of assault. Slavers and nonslavers had been known to satisfy their own desires using Black bodies without consent and at times in horrifically brutal ways. Even if there was no legal ownership, white people did not offer Black people autonomy over their bodies and sexuality. One may not even be owned by the person that assaulted them. With the socialization of the racial hierarchy, whites were able to own or take Black sexuality without any repercussions. Stephanie Jones-Rogers the author of *They Were her Property: White Women as Slave Owners in the American South* writes extensively on white women's role in American slavery. Jones-Rogers writes, "On any given day, white women and girls could witness white men and women committing violent acts upon the nude and partially exposed bodies of enslaved people in their households and on their fields" (Jones-Rogers, 2019, p. 83).

My history lessons painted a picture of white male enslavers; however, that was a drastic generalization. History only seemed to mention the rape of enslaved women. Leaving out that people of all genders, nongenders, and all ages were bought and sold for the sexual or reproductive gratification of some, not all, enslavers. One reason AFAB folx have more awareness in the literature is because the physical evidence of pregnancy and childbirth that prove an assault had happened. Foster highlights that "male victims of slave rape left no biological record in the form of offspring" (Foster, 2018, p. 125). Thus, leaving silent the voices of those identified as men and children that did not conceive. There was also an unspoken right that some men felt they had over women and girl's bodies and sexualities. Many people turned a blind eye to their knowledge of white men and boys raping enslaved people. Solomon said that women were forbidden from indulging in the sexual pleasures with enslaved people; however, men were encouraged to seek out sexual gratification with enslaved people (Solomon, 2017). In all actuality, I wouldn't say women were "forbidden from indulging." This misconception was based on a narrative of white women being seen as pure and wholesome and adhering to the social norms of settler sexuality. Having the consequences result in an illegitimate Black child, made it more difficult for them to indulge than their male counterparts. However, they did indulge. "Although by law the status of a child followed that of its mother, in many cases when a white woman had a child who was gathered by an enslaved man, the child was taken away and placed with the local slave community or sold into slavery elsewhere" (Foster, 2018, p. 140). In the chapter, The *Sexual Abuse of Black Men Under American Slavery* (2018), Foster brings to our attention that "Few scholars have viewed the relationship of enslaved men and free white women through the lens of sexual abuse in part because of gendered assumptions about sexual power" (Foster, 2018, p. 136). That men are the ones raping and women are the ones being raped. The truth is that enslaved Black men were sexually assaulted by white people, and this has been mostly ignored. Foster tells us why:

> The rape of slave men has also gone unacknowledged because of the current and historical tendency to define rape along gendered lines, making both victims and perpetrators reluctant to discuss male rape. The sexual assault of men dangerously points out cracks in the marble base of patriarchy that asserts men as penetrators in opposition to the penetrable, whether homosexuals, children, or adult women. This article, therefore, confronts our own raced, classed, and gendered perceptions of rape and argues that we have a moral imperative to recognize the coerced sexuality of enslaved men as rape. Narrowly defining sexual assault along gendered lines has obscured our ability to recognize the climate of terror and the physical and mental sexual abuse that enslaved men also endured.
>
> (Foster, 2018, p. 126)

Pause. Turn your attention inward and check in with your body, mind, and emotions

Not only do we need to alter the gendered perceptions around rape, but we also need to revisit how we look at sexual assault. Thomas Foster tells us that the forms of abuse suffered by Black men during slavery can be documented through accounts of "penetrative assault, forced reproduction, sexual coercion and manipulation, and psychic abuse" (Foster, 2018, p. 125). The toll exists beyond the physical body and our definition needs to take into account the psychic toll produced from the gaslighting that was plaguing the sexualities of enslaved people. "All the while being portrayed as sexually dangerous, the real danger sexually dangerous, the real danger was really coming from the ones spinning the story. That is manipulation and a trauma of epic proportion. It's up to us to challenge, dismantle, and reconstruct our definition of sexual assault, with the consideration on expanding its definition to include other nonphysical types of sexual harm. In this text, we are not going to argue whether an enslaved person offered consent to someone in positions of power over them. Manipulation, coercion, and threats set aside we cannot overlook the fact that at times, in many sexual scenarios, enslavers posed, "Legal ownership that enabled control of the enslaved body" (Foster, 2018). Yes, there have been loving relationships between enslaved people and nonenslaved people. The argument comes when we say they have given full consent when enslaved people hold limited power in the relationship and socially and may be dependent on their lover in some way for survival.

Pause

Turn inward. Be still so you can listen within. Tend to yourself and your needs. "Scribe," move, hum, sing. When you are ready, you can continue on to the next section.

We are moving back into historical racialized sexual trauma, when Black bodies were forced into reproduction, and enslaved people were bred as if they were livestock. For some Black men, they were given a specific role in this trade. Those possessing genetic traits seen as desirable by enslavers were used as "stud," "bull," or "stockmen." Forced to have sex with many women for the sake of reproducing strong offspring that could be born into servitude. This, of course, became especially popular when the transatlantic slave trade was shut down, and it became illegal to export humans from another country for free labor. The need for increasing the population of enslaved people in America to keep the economy going added an additional reproductive motivation when buying and selling people. Foster highlights that "Forcing some enslaved men to reproduce with many different women denied to them a fatherly role even while it prevented their children from bonding with them" (Foster, 2018, p. 133). Controlling sexuality for reproduction became yet another means for control of the Black body and it worked as an agent to dismantle the African American kinship structures. Children were often sold alone. Standing, if they were old enough, on an auction block without any of their relations. Baptist notes, "From 1815 to 1820, in fact, New Orleans saw 2,646 sales of children under the age of thirteen, of whom 1, 001 were sold separately from any other family member. Their average age was nine, many were younger—some much younger" (Baptist, 2014, p. 106).

Dr Degruy writes:

> Historically, African societies were arranged and based upon kinship rela-
> tionships. The extended family was an interdependent unit that provided
> for the care of the children, the sick, and the elderly. In African culture
> your nieces and nephews would consider themselves brothers and sisters
> instead of cousins. The extended family structure was part of a survival
> strategy, particularly for Africans whose kinship ties provided the mecha-
> nism for child-rearing and social organization. The members of the ex-
> tended family help to provide for the basic needs of food, clothing, and
> shelter. Family cooperation [was for] the survival of a tribe or group.
>
> (Degruy, 2017)

Many Africans came from a matrilineal tribe and then they were displaced in
a colonial patriarchal structure where what it meant to be a man was interwoven in the ability to protect your women and children. However, Black men
were often stripped of their ability to protect. In order to establish full control
of the female Black body, men would exert their power by removing partners and other kinships that may help their female victims (Baptist, 2014).
Men were not only sexually assaulted themselves, but were also helpless
bystanders witnessing the sexual abuse of women and children. They were
unable to adhere to the colonial patriarchal standard of being a "man" by
protecting their most defenseless. "Slavery violated the masculinity of black
men who were denied the ability to protect vulnerable female dependents"
(Foster, 2018, p. 124). Bystander trauma occurs when an individual watches
someone go through a traumatic event. Foster writes that the accumulation
of the bystander trauma took an "emasculating psychic toll" on these men
(Foster, 2018, p. 124).

Dr. Joy Degruy speaks of this psychic toll for parents that witnessed the
sexual assault of their children:

> This mother knows there will be a day when white men will demand to
> have access to her daughter and that these men or boys will use for fragile
> young body to satisfy their sexual cravings. That day may mark the initia-
> tion into manhood for the slave master's son, or perhaps that day she will
> be offered as any evening gift for white male visitors. The mother no doubt
> anguishes over this fact but still she hopes to lessen the tragic event by at
> least acquainting her innocent child with the particulars of being raped.
> She tries to help her little girl understand what will happen and why it's
> happening at all. She endeavors to explain how it will feel, how her vagina
> will tear, burn, and bleed. She attempts to tell her how best to prepare and
> survive the ordeal; tells her to lie still, not to resist, and try to bear the pain.
> But there are limits to what you can tell the child to better prepare for. She
> cannot tell her how often they will come, how long it will last, or how

many there will be. This mother cannot protect her. Nor can the father, who looks on powerless, defeated, and emasculated.

(Degruy, 2017)

It can be assumed that not only people in the Black community were experiencing bystander trauma but there were many also were many white settlers witnessing these sexual traumas of Black people. White people were able to fulfill their sexual desires with everything that fell outside the confines of settler sexuality on their human property in more ways than physical rape. "Whipping exposed male flesh carried a homoerotic charge—one that mirrored the nearly obscene fixation on whipping nude enslaved woman" (Foster, 2018, p. 128). Many of this was done in public view. There is no doubt that nonconsensual sadism was given an outlet to explore and quench erotic longings.

Again, enslavement was matrilineal—a child born to an enslaved woman was born into slavery. There were times when the child would stay with the mother; however, Baptist points out, "The ideal hand did not come with a family. Slave sellers and buyers conspired to break attachments between parents and children" (Baptist, 2014, p. 106). This was largely due to the fact that "A woman who was alone would waste none of her labor on children" (Baptist, 2014, p. 106). Meanwhile, men were almost always sold in solitude, without any familial kinship. Thus, further dismantling the familial safety and tribal kinships. Creating an even greater divide between the connections to their home, land, language, and their image of self. With this practice of "studding" out humans, there was a reinforcement of the hypersexualized Black man stereotype that skimmed the narratives of colonial days. Fear increased of Black men having sex with white women, yet they used the Black men's sexuality to forcibly have sex with Black women. This trope of the Black male sexual savage that can't be controlled, permeated fear and exacerbated the need to protect white women. Foster writes, "The psychic toll was also high. Being told that one is hypersexual and uncontrollable cannot be dismissed as mere racist caricaturing; for some men, such messages would have inflicted great emotional pain" (Foster, 2018, p. 129). When the "stockmen" aged out of their best reproductive years, they were no longer of use. If a man was seen as "undesirable" for breeding, they controlled his sexuality in such a way that would prevent him from reproducing.

Pause

What are you feeling in your body now? Is it warm, cold, or in between? Is it tense or relaxed? Take a moment to take a deep breath and relax any tension you feel in your jaw, shoulder, arms, and legs.

When you are ready, we will continue with another form of abuse found within enslaved breeding: forced coupling. This was forcing a man and a woman into domestic and nonconsensual marital or sexual unions.

"Scholarly Focus has generally viewed these forced couplings from the point of view of the assaulted woman, often wholly neglecting the male participant" (Foster, 2018, p. 132). The sexual trauma that men endured through forced coupling is rarely seen in scholarship.

> Continuing to overlook the victimization of men in such sexual assaults not only denies the full extent of that sexual abuse but also continues dangerously to draw on long-standing stereotypes of black male sexuality that positions black men as hyper sexual.
>
> (Foster, 2018, p. 133)

Many men were forced into marriages where their partners did not consent to be with them. They were forced to have sex, at times at gunpoint, to impregnate their unwilling wife. "For such men, the rejection and resentment of their forced wives would have further compounded their dehumanizing situation." As I mentioned in Chapter 3, at the end of slavery, you can find a trend of people separating from their forced relationship and some searching for their true partners (Foster, 2018). If the quasimarriage resulted in impregnation and managed to carry to full term, the lingering question may be "What happens to our baby?"

The Grammy award-winning artist Rhiannon Giddens writes and sings of the complicated lives of Black people in the colonial days with what I'm calling modern plantation music. She speaks openly of her music being influenced by her research on colonization. Moved by books such as *The Slaves War: The Civil War in the Words of Former Slaves* by Andrew Ward, she processed and channeled her pain into her music. On her NPR Tiny Desk appearance, she discusses the origins of the song "At the Purchaser's Option," which she wrote after she saw an ad in the book for a young enslaved woman. At the end of the ad, there was mention of the woman having a nine-month-old baby that "was at the purchaser's option" (NPR Music, 2019). Giddens introduced this song by saying, "In thinking about this young woman, how could she get up every morning knowing that none of her life, including her own children was under her control" (NPR Music, 2019). I encourage you to search up the song on YouTube. The song talks of being raped at a young age and becoming a woman as she transitions into motherhood with the resulting child. It speaks of childhood sexual assault, losing childhood too soon, combined with the ambiguous anxiety, fear, and sadness surrounding the uncertainty in her ability to keep her own child and what the future may look like for them. All the while, she must get up every day and provide free manual labor.

Another form of historical sexualized and racialized trauma is the medical trauma experienced by BILPOC folx. You probably have already heard of James Marion Sims and the experimental surgeries he performed on enslaved women that struggled with obstetric vesicovaginal fistulas. Vesicovaginal fistulas are normally formed during laboring trauma, where a tear or opening occurs between the vagina and bladder that can cause urinary incontinence. Three victims of Sims have been named in the literature, Lucy, Anarcha, and Betsey with many more unnamed people. He is known now for performing repeated surgeries on enslaved women without any anesthesia. "Sims reasoned that these women were able to bear great pain because their race made them more durable, and thus they were well suited for painful experimentation" (Degruy, 2017, p. 61). I'm uncertain whether he actually believed, or he just told himself, and his colleagues that Black people did not feel pain in the same ways that white people did. Sims is said to have performed 30 surgeries alone on Anarcha without anesthesia. What is commonly left out of the story is that he developed these innovations for the field of obstetrics on the backs of enslaved women. After some time, when his white colleagues refused to take part in his grotesque practice, he trained other enslaved women as surgical assistants, and had them hold down each other while he performed the surgeries. After mastering his techniques, he conducted this surgery on white women with anesthesia. Sims was celebrated as the godfather of gynecology for his advancements of the first surgery to repair these fistulas and for developing the pap smear speculum. These atrocities became public when activists fought to have the removal of his statue from Central Park in New York.

An additional part to Sims's story that I learned long after he was praised in my own Human Sexuality course was the experimental surgeries he did on Black babies with neonatal tetanus. This was a condition from unsanitary living conditions that created malformations in the skull. "Sims attributed the condition to the indecency and intellectual flaws of blacks" (Degruy, 2017, p. 63). Sims used the condition as an opportunity to perform more experimental surgeries. "Sims attempted to treat this malady by trying to pry the bones in the skulls of tiny infants into alignment with the use of a shoemaker's awl" (Degruy, 2017, p. 63). Reproduction and maternal care were weaponized against Black bodies. Degruy points out, "Slavery provided wealthy white citizens the ability to purchase a virtually endless supply of men, women, and children to abuse in whatever manner their fancies bid them, for however long the enslaved could survive; and all with total impunity" (Degruy, 2017, p. 63).

Pause

Breath, slow, feel, ground and scribe. Continue when you are ready.

Remember the questions from the reflection in the beginning of this chapter? What do you see when you envision an enslaver? How do you see their age, gender, and race in your imagination? I wanted you to reflect on your automatic thoughts and images that arise when you picture an enslaver in your mind. There is a common misconception that white male enslavers were the sole perpetrators of sexual violence throughout the colonial days. Many people and media exclude white women from their preconceived notions of who an enslaver was. When I asked you in the beginning of this chapter to imagine an enslaver, did you omit women from your imagery? If you imagined women, what was their role? What did they look like? The reality is that women were indeed enslavers. Jones-Rogers writes, "Slave-owning women not only witnessed the most brutal features of slavery, they took part in them, profited from them, and defended them" (Jones-Rogers, 2019, p. xi). There are several reasons why white women are not portrayed accurately in the literature. Jones-Rogers points out that people carry this assumption that "women's legal status as wives prevented them from owning slaves in their own right and married women merely lived in households in which they engaged with, managed, and benefited from the labor of the enslaved people that others owned" (Jones-Rogers, 2019, p. xi). The truth is that both single and married white women could hold claim to their own enslaved people. There were two main markets that white women were interested in as Jones-Rogers explains. White women were involved in the slave hiring markets to obtain both "enslaved wet nurses and other kinds of enslaved laborers" (p. 112). Wet nurses were lactating people that were bought or hired to chestfeed white babies human milk. "In the context of southern slave markets, and slave mothers' breast milk was a commodity that could be bought and sold, and buyers and sellers recognize these woman's ability to suckle as a form of largely invisible yet skilled labor" (Jones-Rogers, 2019, p. 114). Selling and renting out wet nurses created a market tailored to white mothers to profit from. A woman that sells "fresh" human milk would add additional income and status within their communities. The demand that white women created for human milk was as Jones-Rogers writes, "crucial to the further commodification of enslaved women's reproductive bodies, through the appropriation of their breast milk and the nutritive and maternal care they provided to white children" (Jones-Rogers, 2019, p. 102). The demand among slave-owning women for enslaved wet nurses transformed the ability to suckle into a skilled form of labor, and created a largely invisible niche sector of the slave market that catered exclusively to white women" (Jones-Rogers, 2019, p. 102). Jones-Rogers makes clear white women's role as profiteer of this niche sector. White women were very much involved if not in control of some enslaved people's human milk.

Jones-Rogers' research found many advertisements for wet nurses. Some advertisements would detail the wet nurses' loss of children. She writes, "There was an important reason individuals mentioned an enslaved woman's loss in their advertisements: their lack of children was a selling point. Individuals routinely placed advertisements that express the desire to hire or purchase a wet nurse without children" (Jones-Rogers, 2019, p. 119). Ads would list "birth order and ages of the enslaved wet nurse's children" to highlight if she had "young" or "fresh breast milk." Knowing if a wetnurse was being sold alone, with children, and the ages of children "offered interested parties' important details to help them determine whether the advertised labor would suit their needs" (Jones-Rogers, 2019, p. 119). Jones-Rogers also found ads describing these women's mental health as either having a "good deposition" or having the "sulks" (Jones-Rogers, 2019, p. 119). If a woman lost her child and struggled with grief and loss, she had the "sulks," and her value would decrease. Jones-Rogers writes, "The slaveholding household was a place of coerced production and reproduction, racial and sexual exploitation, and physical and psychological violence" (Jones-Rogers, 2019, p. 83). She points out that these slaveholding households were "a place where white women grew accustomed to the violence of slavery, contemplated the sale and purchase of slaves, and used the bodies of the enslaved people they owned in ways that reinforced their pecuniary value" (Jones-Rogers, 2019, p. 83).

Women where not the only victims of white women. One can find several written accounts of white women coercing or sexually exploiting Black men (Foster, 2018). Foster writes, "The traditional denial of white women's sexual agency has contributed to our obscured view of those white women who sexually assaulted and exploited enslaved men" (Foster, 2018, p. 134). The trend to ignore the sexual trauma enslaved men experienced is because "the abuse of black men at the hands of white woman stands on its head the traditional gendered views of racial and sexual assault" (Foster, 2018). The narrative was and still is that Black men rape white women, not the other way around. Though, there is evidence that white women were not innocent from sexually assaulting enslaved people. When looking at the relationship white women had with enslaved folx, Foster points out,

> It was understood that white women at times took the initiative in interracial sex is not, of course, in itself evidence of the sexual abuse of enslaved men, although it's worth repeating that the enslaved status of black men in such interactions made them necessarily vulnerable.
>
> (Foster, p. 134)

It is difficult to argue enthusiastic consent when a person is owned. Foster hypothesizes that some white women were able to remain single and stay virtuous in the public eye by maintaining secret sexual relationships with enslaved men, "Some white women initiated sexual encounters and made clear what they wanted, knowing that their cultural role, the sexual innocence expected of them, helped to hide their actions" (p. 134). White women had the perfect cover, the portrayal of innocence, to get away with their sexual crimes. There is some historical evidence demonstrating enslaved people in loving relationships with white folx; however, Jones-Rogers cautions, "no matter how affectionate relations between white girls and enslaved people might have been, these young slave owners frequently articulated and exercise their power over their enslaved companions as mistresses in the making" (Jones-Rogers, 2019, p. 17).

There is also evidence that enslaved men were paid for sex with white women that were not their owners (Foster, 2018). Foster tells us that "Enslaved men, like enslaved women, may well have negotiated opportunities that sex under slavery presented them to their advantage" (Foster, p. 143). With these opportunities, it was common to see, "direct threats or indirect manipulation, with a more subtle threat of violence, accompanied some of these relationships" (Foster, 2018, p. 134).

Pause. Feel. Tune in. Breath. Relax. Scribe. Continue on when you are ready

The continuation of slave rape of epic proportions grew a population of majority paternally white mixed with maternal Black people that were born in bondage. I mentioned earlier that these mixed-race people at the time were called "mulatto," which broadly meant having both Black and white heritage. However, it could have also included Indigenous heritage. Due to colorism, texturism, featurism, and other European standards of beauty, these mixed-race people were favored for sexual exploitation. While sexual assault was enacted upon enslaved people of all shades, there was the phenomenon of monopolizing the sexual attraction of mixed-race people. Baptist wrote extensively on the "Fancy Trade." He writes, "Starting in the early 1830s, the term 'fancy girl' or 'maid' began to appear in the marketing of the interstate slave trade. It meant a young woman, usually light-skinned, sold at a high price explicitly linked to her sexual availability and attractiveness" (Baptist, 2014, p. 240). The proximity to whiteness that the mixed-race people had was deemed more sophisticated, attractive, and sexy. As mentioned above, Black women had been subjected to the sexualized slave markets—"but what was now emerging was different." The fancy traded created a sexualized marketing campaign that "branded and marketed the ability to coerce sexuality, priming white entrepreneurs to believe that the purchase of enslaved-people-as commodities offered white men freedoms not found in ordinary life." Promotion of sex with a "yellow miss" influenced travel for sex. The term "fancy branded slavetrading as sexy for sellers and buyers" (Baptist, 2014, p. 243). Baptiste discusses more on long-term sex work arrangements white men would have with mixed-race women called "placage" (Baptist, 2014, p. 238).

Women were not the only commodity when it came to the fancy trade. Baptist and Foster both discuss the "Fancy" trade by looking at the mixed-race men that were used for the sexual satisfaction of white people. "The evidence also leads us to speculate that unusual interest in light-skinned men may have paralleled the more formalized documented fetish market in 'fancy maids.'" Foster (2014) writes,

> Such testimony raises the possibility that in this patriarchal society the sexual abuse of "nearly white" men could enable white women to enact radical fantasies of domination over white men with the knowledge that their victim's body was legally black and enslaved, subject to the women's control.
>
> (Foster, 2014, pp. 127–128)

Without evidence, one could speculate that there was also a market for children in the fancy markets. Just as there have been gendered concepts of abuse clouding the reality, we too have dismissed enslaved assaults to have occurred not only to just women, but adult women. Leaving the stories of countless children that were bought, sold, and rented for sexual gratification was another facet of slavery that was masked by gendered and ageist conceptions of rape and abuse.

Reflection

How does reading about this portion of North American history sit in your body?

How has this chapter been similar or different to others you have read around enslaved African sexuality?

Was there something new you learned about American history as it pertains to sexuality?

What other part have been left out?

Can you see any parallels between these historical trends and what we see today?

4 Oya

The Orisha Oya protects the realm between life and death. She is said to shepherd the deceased to the afterlife. A symbol of change sometimes seen holding a machete, she is known to clear stagnation from paths to make room for new growth. I invite you to clear stagnation from your path and make room for a more fertile re-growth.

In his book *My Grandmother's Hands: Racialized Trauma and the Pathway to Mending Our Hearts and Bodies*, Resmaa Menekeem offers a guide to look at how the historical trauma of our ancestors are impacting us today. In Chapter 3, we discussed the historical sexual trauma that enslaved Africans endured in colonial America. This chapter will explore how the historical sexual trauma lives on in our bodies and psyche. Menekeem shows us that it is a combination of "genes, history, culture, laws, and family" that impacts the trauma stored in Black bodies. He goes on to say, "That trauma then becomes the unconscious lens through which they view all of the current experiences" (p. 13). Sexual trauma too can shape this "unconscious lens" and influence sexual decision-making, cognitions, and feelings. They have impacted policies, laws, and the systems we are a part of. Menekeem refers to trauma as a "wordless story." We can't tap into it with words, thoughts, or cognitions. Repeatedly, this unspoken trauma keeps getting passed down generation after generation. This chapter assists the reader in identifying how some of the ethnosexual historical traumas impact modern-day American sexual behavior and draw connections to present-day Black bodies.

Before we start, take a breath. Inhale deeper than you have all day and fill your lungs with air. Now, take three deep breaths, each one deeper than the last. On the last one, make an audible sigh, if that is comfortable for you now.

In Chapter 3, I discussed some of the atrocities that shaped North American sexuality, highlighting historical sexual trauma. This chapter assists the reader in identifying some ethnosexual historical traumas and their impact on modern-day American sexual behavior. The impact of being removed from your country and kinships in violent ways and involuntary ways has lasting influences on people. Few people have examined how the associated trauma

DOI: 10.4324/9781003276951-5

greatly impacted the African and later African American people's sexuality. Resmaa Menekeem offers a guide to looking at how the historical trauma of our ancestors are impacting all of us today. He writes, "Our very bodies house the unhealed dissonance and trauma of our ancestors" (p. 10). After reading his text, I used my lens as a sexologist to hypothesize that the historical racialized and sexualized trauma too is stored in our bodies, which, over time, created generalized responses in people that have significant impacts on the relationships and the sexuality of us all. Resmaa explains that it is a combination of "genes, history, culture, laws, and family" that impact the trauma stored in our bodies. As a sex therapist, I have been given a bird's eye view into how we all hold wounds about ourselves, our bodies, and our sexualities. Resmaa feels that we hold the accumulated consequences inside ourselves. He writes, "While we see anger and violence in the streets of our country, the real battlefield is inside our bodies. If we are to survive as a country, it is inside our bodies where this conflict will need to be resolved" (Menekeem, xvii). Trauma does not only exist in our cognitive brains. It becomes the "unconscious lens" through which we "view all of our current experiences" (p. 13). My thoughts are that it is this same "unconscious lens" that also filtering our sexual experiences. These "wordless stories" can't be accessed with words or cognitions. Repeatedly, the embedded trauma keeps getting passed down, generation after generation.

> There is something about our society that tends to allow or legitimize certain forms of violence toward certain people. In this way, we are all survivors and/or descendants of survivors of trauma. We learn to adapt either by avoiding the trauma, healing the trauma, or victimizing ourselves or others.
>
> (Archer p. 88)

David archer, the author of *Anti-racist Psychotherapy: Confronting Systemic Racism and Healing Racial Trauma* is attuned to the impacts of trauma on both an individual and social level. He writes, "While all forms of suffering are damaging, some appear to leave 'trauma' in the individual and scar our social orders" (Archer, 2021, p. 23). Both Archer and Menekeem speak that the trauma that happens to an individual can scar our communal networks. We will talk more about this in Chapter 5. The ethnosexual trauma scars have impacted all genders and races, yet little has been done to examine and heal these wounded parts of our culture. The healing of Black sexuality does not start and stop with Black people. In order to create a space for Black bodies to heal, white bodies, people of color, and culture need to simultaneously be doing the same. When all of our nervous systems stay regulated in this work, we can collectively come to a grounded and healing place.

Several scholars have worked to define the psychic pains African Americans and Black people experience in modern America. The author of *Back*

Then and Right Now in the History of Psychology: A History of Human Psychology in African Perspectives for the New Millennium, John Oshodi, discusses Maafa, a "collective force of psychopathology in Blacks with features of traumatization, dehumanization, inferiority, and hostility, stemming from the cavity of White supremacy" (Oshodi, 2004, p. 119). You also may have heard of the term coined by Dr Degruy, Post Traumatic Slave Syndrome (PTSS) defined as

> Post traumatic slave syndrome is a condition that exists when a population has experienced multi-generational trauma resulting from centuries of slavery and continues to experience oppression and institutionalized racism today. Added to this condition is the belief (real or imagined) that the benefits of the society in which they live are not accessible to them. This, then, is Post Traumatic Slave Syndrome: Multigenerational trauma Together with continue depression and absence of opportunities access to benefits available in the society leads to . . . Post Traumatic Slave Syndrome.
>
> (p. 105)

Many have highlighted, others have denied, the consequences of settler colonialism on Black bodies. I feel we have insurmountable evidence that white-cis-hetero-patriarchy has dismantled our ancestral kinships, relations to ourselves, land, and sexualities; thus, causing psychological harm for many of us past and present.

There are many fascinating findings around trauma. Please understand that I am by no means a neuropsychologist and I can't say that I completely grasp psychobiology and neuropsychology and all its complexities. Because it seems so complex to me, yet, I know the importance, I try to simplify it when I talk to my clients about their nervous systems. I describe the bagnus the vagus nerve as a column, which is really a long nerve that runs down the trunk of our body. It starts at the brainstem and goes down our center to our colon. I describe these smaller nerves that are interconnected to other organs and parts of our body that branch out and receive information that we are not always cognitively aware of. I also tell them that some people have believed this column to be associated with chakras. While some call it the "wandering nerve," Resmaa calls it our "soul nerve." Calling it the soul nerve, to me, elicits feelings of a more ancient, wiser, and a part of something larger. I believe that we must center the soul nerve in regulating our nervous system to fully process racialized trauma and heal.

I have been unfolding, examining, sitting in my own racialized trauma with a new lens enhanced by my academic interests over the last couple of years. This trauma is something that has made me feel stuck. I sometimes weep and feel constricted. I get confused, blown off center, and at times, shrink back, or grow large with intense rage. As I started recognizing and validating my own pain, I realized that many people around me were not ready, maybe they never will be, to have discussions around race that it will take for me to have a trusting and authentic relationship with them. I started to realize how many people do not see or outright deny white supremacy and the privileges and pain associated with it. I think it's harder for me, the closer they are to me. I am often pleasantly surprised when a white person can engage in dialogue that demonstrates some understanding to the complexities POC have to navigate and that they do indeed see it as a privilege they do not have to endure such navigation. I guess I'm surprised when they speak because the majority of white people, I experience here in the PNW and within some institutions I have been involved in, have difficulties engaging in sensitive conversations. Some outright prohibit it. There are people out there fighting right now to keep both Critical Race Theory (CRT) and Sexuality education out of schools. This censorship stunts our studies on ethnosexuality limiting our communal knowledge on both race and sex. I was blind sighted when the suggestion of omitting social justice was brought up in my own work. My friend and colleague Kristen Lilla and myself are American Association Sex Educators Counselors and Therapist (AASECT) continuing education providers. After our last Ethics workshop together, we received this in our anonymous evaluation form, "While we live in an ever-changing cultural context, the hyper focus on this takes away from learning & growing as sexologists . . . very disheartening." The utter denial of the need for discussion around some of these complex issues prevents at worst and slows at best the movement in healing. It still shocks me that when I am in an inclusive space of sexuality professionals, people shame and criticize the attempted movements in diversity, equity, and inclusion (DEI).

This is without a doubt a significant challenge. As many of us live within systems that have no desire for change. Even within spaces where we should be safe to advocate for the well-being of all, there are those who oppose growth and expansion.

Mignolo (2016)
    We, and I mean all of us, queer or not, of color or not, are trapped. The difference is that the creative energy for transformation is coming and will continue to grow, from people racialized/sexualized and not from the side of the racializing/sexualizing. And even when it comes, when white and heterosexual (men and women) of consciousness, from and in the former first world, realize that their thoughts, behavior, belief, knowledge has been imposed upon them and they further realize the injustices that such classificatory social fictions have caused, still they cannot see, know, and experience the colonial wound. And that is fine because there is no, cannot be, universal experience.

(p. xi)

Universal experiences are nearly impossible when considering all of one's identities that create their positionality. As Kimberlé Crenshaw's

Intersectionality framework shows when marginalized identities, like race and gender, collide, there can be compounded stress. For a moment, I would like to talk about when ethnosexuality intersects with gender. First, I have to mention that settler colonialism has had a tight hold on gender since its inception. Iantaffi writes, "the gender expansiveness of many tribal nations was yet another challenge to Christian, patriarchal hegemony" (Iantaffi, 2021, p. 24); thus, leaving those outside the gender binary boundaries susceptible to colonial harm. When sitting in my racialized trauma, I was invited to simultaneously examine my gender trauma.

When looking back at my own childhood, one thing that really stands out to me is the unsolicited and intrusive questions others would ask me that made me feel like there was a barrier that kept me othered as someone different. Growing up, people were often confused by me having a white mother and relatives. I had grown accustomed to being asked, "are you adopted" all the time. My first memories of the intersection of ethnosexuality and gender was being misgendered as a child and during my adolescence, I presented to others as a boy. I really hated those scratchy dresses from the 1980s with the lace, the stiffness, and worst of all, the tights. It was the ultimate discomfort, and I remember fighting to not wear a dress anytime I was asked to wear one. When my family could get me in a dress, I would routinely hear, "keep your legs shut, so nobody sees up your dress." Trying to keep my knees locked together made my small body feel constricted. Aside from my clothes, my mother did not know how to take care of my full mane of curls and had my hair cut to about one inch all over. Even though I hated my hair cut short and would cry when it was cut, my mother would tell me, "Well, you don't like to have your hair brushed." The truth was, she didn't know how to tend to it (Figure 4.1). I remember being envious of straight hair that looked as though it hardly had to be brushed and it laid down smooth and long. On a playdate at my house, I remember seeing my mom grab a pinch of my white friend's hair softly and stroking the piece till she reached the ends. I twinged with jealousy. To this younger part of myself, hair was a measure of a beauty I could not achieve. I was told my hair was "frizzy" or unmanageable and shown through 1980s media that beauty was, at its core, whiteness. Long straight hair emboldened a sense of femininity I was longing to be recognized for. Despite having earrings in both ears, which I thought would assure everyone I was indeed a girl, the other question I was always asked was "are you a boy or a girl?" I could see other children, and sometimes adults, sizing me up. They might be thinking I didn't look like a "girl." There is a specific color for girls, pink. "She's not wearing pink. Girls wear dresses. She's not wearing a dress. Girls have long hair. Her hair is short. Got it. She's a boy. We better ask to make sure." The misgendering left a wound on my sexual self. The gender wound grew larger creating more disembodiment when working in tandem with racism and white cis-hetero-normative standards of beauty that were pervasive at the time. If there weren't strict colonial standards to which a little girl could exist in her gender, this trauma would not have existed.

Figure 4.1 Anne around six years old posing for a picture with one hand holding up her
head while lying on a log in front of a lake. She has short curly hair, she is
wearing a blue jacket and jeans, a pair of white tennis shoes, and her nails
are painted.

When I look at the distress that other people's perceptions had of my intersecting identities, I ask myself, "what are the historical, political, legal, and
representation" themes associated with this discomfort, and, of course, they
trace back to settler colonialism. When looking at gender or sexual orientation
harm, I think of the term "Covert Cultural Sexual Abuse" coined by Joe Kort.
In his book *LGBTQ Clients in Therapy: Clinical Issues and Treatment*, he explains, "The psychological consequences of microaggressions, homophobia,
and heterosexism parallel those of sexual abuse. The trauma not only affects
psychological identity but also negatively influences psychosexual formation
and identity" (Kort, 2018). Kort says that the accumulation of all this harm
"parallel those of sexual abuse."

When I consider racialized trauma, gender trauma, and sexual orientation
trauma, I think of Resmaa reminding us that shared trauma within a community over time can look like culture. We have built a culture around unhealed
sexual trauma, which can inhibit or prohibit certain responses to sexual stim-
uli. Including being complicit with the sexual harm of certain people.

As mental health professionals, we are trained in using the Diagnostic
and Statistical Manual of Mental Disorders (DSM); however, this guidebook
leaves no room for the nuances and complexities we see in the trauma showing up in our therapeutic spaces. You don't see the trauma of surviving white

supremacy, incarceration trauma, financial/poverty trauma, bystander trauma, medical, racialized (historical and present), transgenerational, multigeneration, intergenerational, religious, gender, complex, or covert sexual abuse showing up in DSM. The creative that seeks reimbursement will extrapolate numbers and codes and attach them to a person that best serves their presenting problems, such as other Specified Trauma/Stressor Related Disorder (309.89). Many conditions, observed behaviors, and phenomena cannot be formally diagnosed. There is not a space that exists in this manual that represents the accumulation of harm. When we don't have a criterion for racialized harm in the DSM, we are acting as agents in ignoring its psychological impacts on the therapeutic community. In order to see the outcomes that many of us desire in liberation from colonial harm, we must examine the racist underbelly of American culture within our profession. The same binaries that have divided us on a hierarchy of race are those that divide us in gender, ability, class, and sexual orientation to name a few. The historical background of the DSM demonstrates the perpetuation of settler harm. Exploration is needed to emancipate us from its limiting confines.

5 Ori

Ori, the head, our destiny, the creator inside us all.

Please take a deep breath. Actually, make that three. With each breath slightly deeper than the one before and the third being the deepest you have taken all day. When you find tightness or construction you can use the breath to stretch and expand. I invite you to use breathwork to keep you grounded. This is a gentle reminder that the following will include the subject of sexual violence. Take a pause when you need to.

Reflections

Take a moment to journal about the following questions:
How have you seen Black bodies sexually exploited in the present day?
How have Black bodies been portrayed in erotica and porn?
What are common sexualized stereotypes of Black people and bodies?
How have you seen Black bodies adorned or celebrated?

When it comes to the aftermath of colonization on Black bodies, I think some things can be easily seen and understood yet many are not so tangible. A general understanding of historical trends, present-day policies, and proceedings can lead a person to see how deeply racist and harmful our history is and how our present day is still blindly grasping at its concepts. Mignolo (2016) reminds us that "Racism and sexism always work together for people of color." Here are some examples of the intersection of racism and sexism with sexual violence.

The Missing and Murdered Indigenous Women, Girls, and Two-Spirit People (MMIWG2S+) epidemic and the need for the #MeToo movement are desperate signals of the continuation of sexual violence stemming from our colonial past. The MMIWG2S+ social movement was started in Canada as First Nations activists demanded Prime Minister Justin Trudeau to take action on an inquiry of their lost loved ones. What the inquiry found was that their "solen sisters" were being taken, sexually assaulted, and murdered at alarming rates. A fact I'm sure the First Nation people were long aware of, however, this brought it into media view and brought awareness to non-Indigenous people. With growing loss and

DOI: 10.4324/9781003276951-6

frustrations of the murdered and missing Native American loved ones, here in the United States, The Urban Health Institute: A division of the Seattle Indian Health Board launched their own study with the mission of "decolonizing data, for Indigenous people, by Indigenous people" to find answers to eradicate this epidemic. With limited funding, they collected data from as many states within the United States as they could, but they were unable to reach them all, however, they reached 29. You can find a PDF of their report on their website: www.uihi. org/. The first page in bold letters says, "Due to Urban Indian Health Institute's limited resourced and the poor data collection by numerous cities, the 506 cases identified in this report are likely an undercount." There are many barriers to American Indian and Alaska native (AI/NA) people reporting sexual crimes. The culture of sexual abuse leaves them with little support both legally and emotionally. The findings show that out of the 5,712 MMIW reported in 2016, only 116 cases were logged into the US Department of Justice's federal missing persons database. UIHI found themes that were assisting in the sexual violence against American Indian and Alaska Native (AI/AN) "poor relationships be-tween law enforcement and American Indian and Alaska Native communities, poor record-keeping protocols, institutional racism in the media, and a lack of substantive relationships between journalists and American Indian and Alaska Native communities." We know that many of these crimes are happening on reservations, and the majority of the perpetrators are nonnatives. Non-Indige-nous people cannot be prosecuted on a reservation and a very small number of reported crimes are actually brought to Federal court. As I currently reside on the Coast Salish Peoples territory, specifically, the unceded Duwamish territory, I sit with the fact that out of the top ten cities that have the highest cases of MMIWG2S+, Seattle ranked number one. The city is named after Chief Si'ahl of the Duwamish tribe. It is disheartening to know that his people are still vic-tims of settler colonialism, genocide, and sexual violence and the majority of our community has never even heard of the MMIW. My office, in Tacoma, WA, sits on the Puyallup Tribe of Indians' land. Tacoma ranks seventh of the top ten cites. Of the top ten states with the most cases of MMIWG2S+, Washington ranks second. The UIHI found disturbingly biased themes presented in the me-dia, "If the case is covered in the media, the language that is used to describe the crime and the victim often causes additional harm." With the lack of reporting and the bias in coverage, the UIHI pleas for, "standards and protocol" to be es-tablished when covering MMIWG2S+ cases, "to decrease the amount of violent language used." This matriarchal movement was created by Indigenous people to protect Indigenous women, then girls, and now Two-Spirit people.

The #MeToo founder Tarana Burke, started the movement in 2017 with the intention of eradicating sexual violence from the lives of People of Color. On her TedTalk, she says:

This is a movement about the 1 and 4 girls and 1 and 6 boys who are sexu-ally assaulted every year and carry those wounds into adulthood. It's about the 84% of trans women who will be sexually assaulted this year. And the Indigenous women who are 3 and half times more likely to be sexually assaulted than any other group. Or, people with disabilities that are 7 times more likely to be sexually abused. It's about the 60% of Black girls like me that will be experiencing sexual violence before the age of 18.

(Ted, 2019)

According to a 2014 study, about 22 percent of Black women reported being raped and 41 percent experienced other forms of sexual violence. For every Black woman that reports her rape, at least 15 Black women do not report theirs (Bureau of Justice Statistics Special Report, Hart & Rennison, 2003. U.S. Department of Justice). Thus, we do not have accurate data on sexual violence on Black women. Burke has been both challenged and threatened for her advocacy efforts to "Dismantle the building block of sexual violence: power and privilege" (Ted, 2019). This matriarchal movement too acknowledges power differentials that perpetuate harm to those that don't have it. Burke says the #MeToo movement offers, "access to a healing journey. To make sure the most marginalized amongst us have an opportunity to start the pathway to healing from the trauma of sexual violence" (Me Too Movement, 2018). What both of these movements have in common is radical community healing. "We believe that communities need to come together to protect the most vulnerable from sexual violence" (Me Too Movement, 2018). Burke discusses the importance of using empathy as tool of empowerment to bring individuals together in radical community healing that will strengthen the individual and the collective. "We want to teach people how to lean into their joy so that they can move away from the trauma and that we can, as a collective, interrupt sexual violence wherever it lives" (Me Too Movement, 2018).

Another area where we see the violence on Black women is in maternal care. Black women have the highest disparities in prenatal care, and they are three to four times more likely to die during childbirth than their white counterparts. Native American birthers are twice as likely. Black birthing bodies are less likely to be seen and heard by their medical care providers. Complaints of pain are discounted due to a long-standing myth that Black people have a higher pain tolerance than their white counterparts. This harm also has consequences on children. Black babies die at three times that of their white counterparts; however, their mortality is increased, if they are birthed by a Black doctor. Black babies also have a lower birth weight, greater chances of childhood obesity, early menses, and cervical cancer.

Women of color (WOC) are far from the only survivors of violence in our communities. The following statistic comes from the 2010 National Intimate Partner (IP) and Sexual Violence Study. They found the prevalence rates of rape, physical violence, and/or stalking against a man by an intimate partner in their lifetime in different racial identities. A total of 3 percent of Asian/Pacific Islander men are survivors of IP. A total of 7.4 percent Hispanic/Latinx, 7.5 percent white,

9 percent mixed race, 12 percent Black, and 12.4 percent AI/AN. I am reminded of Fosters work "Without recognizing male sexual abuse, we run the risk of reinscribing the very stereotypes used by the white slave owners and others who reduced black men to bestial sexual predators and white women to passionless and passive vessels" (Foster, 2018, p. 141). Another important consideration is that Black people make up only 13 percent of the population, however, they "account for nearly 36% of state and federal prisoners" (Degruy, 2005, 2017). We know that if an African American man is convicted of raping a white woman, he will "receive more serious sanctions than all other sexual assault defendant" (Wriggins, 1983). There have been discussions around Black people being disproportionately incarcerated in the United States. While we may be aware of this as a culture, we hardly ever talk about how this is affecting the sexualities of those incarcerated and for those who are being released. Assisting relationships with intimacy after incarceration was never discussed in my training.

Pause Fill your lungs up with air. Feel any sensations as they arise and dissipate. Is there a part of your body that needs care? Breath into that space. If you feel nothing, breathe into the nothingness. If you identify a sensation, offer that part of you something it needs, movement, stretch, dance, moan, hum, jump, hold, and squeeze. Let this part of your body know that you acknowledge the sensations that occurred and that are occurring now. Invite this part to give you a message. Take a writing utensil (please don't type) and paper and use your writing hand to scribe what this part would like to say to you. Don't try to make it make sense. This does not need to make sense. This is a means to tap into the historical and present pain that lives within without words. Using logic to think our way out won't do.

Now, I would like to discuss further some of the impacts of incarceration on sexuality. For the purposes of this book, I have identified sexual trauma from incarceration to contain one or more of the following:

- An individual missed socially acceptable psychosocialsexual developmental milestones due to incarceration.
- Survivor, perpetrator, or bystander of sexual violence that caused incarceration.
- Survivor, perpetrator, or bystander of sexual violence that occurred within detainment, jails, and prisons.
- Incarcerated person's sexual behaviors are not congruent with how the person would live their sexual life on the outside and this causes them significant distress.

Case

Jamar (he/him) a 42-year-old Black cis-man was incarcerated for 25 years shortly after meeting Tiffany (she/her) when he was 16 years old. Tiffany is 40-year-old cis-women that is bi-racial, mixed with Black and Japanese, was

14 years old when they met. During Jamar's incarceration, they had stayed connected through the years with an occasional letter or call. Meanwhile, Tiffany had two consecutive significant relationships during his 25 years in prison and had a child with one of those partners. When Jamar was released two years ago, they reconnected. Tiffany conceived the first time they had sex and their child was born last year. For the duration of their two-year relationship, they have had sex six times. They describe all of the incidences riddled with worry, doubt, insecurity, and feeling inadequate to initiate sexual contact or sharing in mutual pleasure. Both partners felt sexually rejected and neither of them had the skills to communicate about what was happening for each of them. Soon resentment boiled and desires waned and the only conversations being had around sex ended in yelling or tears, leaving each of them longing for intimacy and connection that seemed beyond their reach. The following is from their first session with me:

Therapist: Alright, now that we have finished up with the logistical stuff and paperwork, I'd like you to know that I have read your intake questionnaires. Thank you both for completing that prior to your appointment, so that I could further understand what is brining you both to therapy. I want to start by asking you why you are wanting to start sex therapy now, in this moment in your relationship?

Tiffany turns to Jamar

Tiffany: Go ahead, babe.

Jamar looks down shamefully before looking up with confidence and locking eyes with Anne.

Jamar: Well, I think the main source of our problems is that I was incarcerated for over twenty years. I missed a lot of things I probably would have learned about relationships and sex.

Tiffany: Yea, but when you say that you make it seem like I got *all* this experience. I was only with two people before you.

Jamar: Listen, I missed a lot. Taking your girlfriend to the movies or the dance or whatever. Ya, know. I didn't have any of that. I was locked up at 16! I am 41 years old and have never dated. Never really communicated sexually with any other woman in my life. Sure, I had sex before getting locked up but I have never had a *real* relationship.

Tiffany: So, I think that is why he really looked to me to know what I was doing because I'm the "relationship expert now" but I don't know what I'm doing any more than he does!

Therapist: Ok, thank you both for sharing this with me. Do you mind telling me how comfortable you are with talking about sex with each other?

They lock eyes with each other and smile nervously.

Tiffany: I will speak for myself; I am not comfortable.
Jamar: Same.
Therapist: Knowing that, I am curious how comfortable are you with talking about sex with me in this space?
Tiffany: I am more comfortable. I am ready to work on this and I think we really need this. I am excited to get started.
Jamar: I'm gonna have to keep it real with y'all. (He loses eye contact with Tiffany and the therapist and locks his gaze on the floor) I am not comfortable . . . *at all*. This is really hard for me. I know it's gotta be done. But, Yea. This is going to be really challenging for me.
Therapist: Thank you for keeping it real with us, Jamar. Since you two aren't really comfortable talking about sex with each other, I can only image how challenging it would be to come in here and talk to a complete stranger about some of these things. While I want to acknowledge your discomfort here, I also want to remind you that I specialize in human sexuality and talking about sex in a clinical and educational setting is what I am trained to do. I am literally talking about sex every day, even on my days, off because someone is always trying to talk to me about sex. (They both gently smile). But, all jokes aside, I encourage you both to be open and honest during our time together, I find that most of the time bringing the truest most authentic parts of ourselves to therapy increases our therapeutic outcomes. Jamar, if you're not comfortable talking about something that comes up in session, please know that you don't have to disclose anything you are uncomfortable talking with us about. It is my hope that you will let us know that you are having some discomfort. We don't want to push you past what you can manage. Does that make sense?
Jamar: Thanks for saying that. I do know that this needs to happen and I appreciate you holding this space for us.

Clinical considerations

- Therapists are encouraged to utilize trauma informed approaches.
- Therapists are encouraged to slow the pacing to meet the person with the least amount of comfort.
- Utilize the EX-PLISSIT model with emphasis on permission and reflection.

- Therapists are encouraged to keep clients within their window of tolerance of distress.
- Build shared language with the clients.

It was important for me to create the space that can hold the vulnerabilities, doubt, shame, and love-starved bodies in my therapeutic space. Tiffany expressed excitement to get started, however, you could see the fear and constriction in Jamar's body and affect. Drawing from the EX-PLISSIT model, I was able to normalize Jamar's discomfort and give him permission to share only what he was comfortable with. Jamar was able to explain that he was not comfortable talking about sex to either of us. Offering permission to disclose as much or as little as he felt was right for him was the foundation to our therapeutic alliance. Lucie Feilding writes, "The beginning of each session is an opportunity to seek permission from a client, to see if they are up to delving into particular content, to ask them what they might wish to work on" (Fielding, 2021, p. 63). I reflected back that I was hearing his discomfort and allowed him the space to review the discussion. Using the EX-PLISSIT model assists us in slowing down and ensuring that our clients feel seen and heard. It also helps the client stay within their window of tolerance as they begin to trust that their emotional and sexual boundaries will not be crossed in the therapy space. To further build the therapeutic alliance, creating a shared language that incorporates both the client's and the clinicians' words, phrases, metaphors, and stories build the scaffolding for how the clients will utilize language with each other after the termination of therapy.

6 Osun

One of the most popular Orishas in the sexological community is Osun as she embodies sexuality to many of us. Nkiru Nzegwu, the author of the chapter "Osunality" in the book African Sexology, shares that Osun is "the divinity of fertility, wealth, joy, sensuality and childbirth, protector of women and giver of children to barren women" (Nzegwu, p. 258). She is known to be very beautiful and often seen in yellow or gold. She is associated with bees, honey, sunflowers, the river, and peacocks.

There is a story that long ago, the orishas once grew frustrated with Olodumare (Creator God) and plotted a rebellion against him. When Olodumare caught wind of what the orishas were planning, he withheld the rain creating a drought on earth. Many orishas tried to reach Olodumare in the heavens to plead for the return of rain. They all failed. One day Osun told the other orishas that she was going to try to fly to Olodumare and request he bring the rain back. They laughed. They thought that she was too feminine and beautiful to complete such a grand task. They scoffed, saying things like, "You can't do that, you might break a nail." Osun took the form of a peacock and shocked them all as she flew up into the heavens. When they saw her rising up toward the sun, they thought surely, she would turn around before she was burned. As she ascended, the heat from the sun became unbearable. As she flies closer and closer to the heavens, the more feathers are burnt from Osun's body. She arrives tired and weary. When Olodumare comes to greet her, he does not recognize her. She does not resemble the beautiful and ornate Osun. She looked like an ugly vulture, the color of ash, with all of her feathers burned off. When he does finally realize that it is truly her, he is shocked. He knew how important her beauty was to her and how symbolic and meaningful it is to her identity. For her to lose what she held dear, her beauty, was such a great sacrifice in Olodumare's eye that he sent Osun flying back to earth with the rain following her. As she flew back those that looked to the sky saw a vulture descending. When they too realized it was Oshun, they were in disbelief that she endured the hardship and sacrificed all to save them. This is a story of perseverance and sacrifice I draw strength from and use as a resource at times. Don't let the beauty and eroticism that oozes out of her like honey distract you from all the Osun represents.

DOI: 10.4324/9781003276951-7

Osun has crossed into popular culture with the help of people like Beyoncé, who happens to embody the same beauty and sensuality we know Osun to possess. In the song "Black Parade," you can hear Osun's name sung by Beyoncé. Layered into the song are also more subtle references to hives and honey, which are symbolic of Osun. Beyoncé is also known to wear the colors of Osun in videos like Hold up or in the musical "Black is King." As sexologists, we have mainly looked at Osun as the embodiment of sensuality, sexuality, fertility, seduction, and pleasure. This has been refreshing to the field, as sex educators, counselors, and therapists have long been aware of the lack of pleasure-based sexuality curriculum. Osunality has been helpful in reframing our patriarchal ways of knowing about sexuality. At its core, Osunality "encourages the treatment of sexual pleasuring and enjoyment as of optional importance" (Nzegwu, p. 261). Unlike patriarchal frameworks, this matriarchal lens does not negate the sexuality of those that do not identify as women. It is for everyone.

For some of us, the start to this work has been grounded in decolonization and anti-colonial practices. Iantaffi puts it simply by writing, "At its heart, decolonization is about breaking free from the oppression of settler colonialism physically and legally" (Iantaffi, 2021, p. 42). This in part can be done with the individual; however, much of it must be done as a collective. Especially when considering the legality of oppression. We can start by "Decentering European practices, knowledge, power and dominance (Iantaffi, 2021, p. 42).

Before reading further, I encourage you to think about what it might look like if you were to move away from the oppression of settler colonialism. What would you have to stop adhering to? What would you let go of? What would you embrace?

Mignolo (2016) highlights the insidious and at times invisible damage that coloniality bestows and challenges us to do more than just resist the colonial legacy.

Coloniality you do not see; it is felt by many people who do not fit the spirit of modernity as perpetrations of wounds inflicted by invisible (until decoloniality made visible) colonial differences. Decolonial healing requires building to re-exist rather than energy to only resist. Resistance implies that you accept the rules of the game imposed upon you, and you resist. Re-existence means that you delink from the rules imposed upon you, you create your own rules communally and, therefore, you re-exist affirming yourself as a human being (p. viii).

This is the time and space to heal ourselves, "de-link," and continue the path of re-existing within the field of sexology. My first publication is a chapter titled *More Than Ebony and Ivory: The complexities of doing sex therapy with interracial couples*, in a book titled, *An Intersectional Approach to Sex Therapy: Centering the lives of Black, Indigenous, Racialized, and People of Color*. I'm proud to be a part of this project, as it was the first of its kind with the collaboration with all BILPOC sex therapist, sexuality educators, and sexuality supervisors, each writing a chapter discussing sex therapy and sexuality education with BILPOC clients and students in mind. This is from the introduction of that text.

> Centering human sexuality with an intersectional lens acknowledges and illuminates the relationship of social oppression and discrimination on Sexual Health and Wellness. In a culture that privileges White, cis-gender, heterosexual, monogamous, and non-kinky identities, those who straddle the boundaries of what is perceived as acceptable or those who all together transcend or reject cultural normative sexuality are often in a position of negotiating authentic identity versus discrimination and stigmatized.
>
> (Malone et al., 2022, p. 4)

The colonial wounds, to some, cannot be denied, but the reality is they are denied daily by many. I share a birthday with Martin Luther King Jr. and like many, I am often inspired by his *I Have a Dream* speech. I too have a dream. That one-day folx do not have to navigate shrinking their authentic selves for any form of oppression or to maintain coloniality.

bell hooks in the book *Salvation: Black People and Love* invites us to considers love as an intervention to healing. hooks writes, "I define love as a combination of care, knowledge, responsibility, respect, trust, and commitment" (Hooks, 2001, p. XVIII). I challenge you to bring in these concepts of love into your own healing and your professional anti-colonial practices. hooks continues, "We cannot effectively resist domination if our efforts to create meaningful, lasting personal and social change are not grounded in a love ethic" (Hooks, 2001, p. XXIV). hooks contends that "Love is our hope and our salvation." (hooks, 2001, p. XXIV). This love also needs to be extended to ourselves.

Healing the personal self

Decolonizing ourselves in part is understanding how we have been adhering to westerncentric standards. One way many of us try to measure up is through productivity. The dominance of westerncentric practices in work-life culture are exhausting. Oshodi writes, "Euro-centric concepts continue to accentuate individuality, independence, materialism, control competitiveness, and differentiation, which collectively further remove the strengths of natural orderliness and harmony from human functioning" (Oshodi, 2004, p. 118). I believe part of the "natural orderliness and harmony" is partially achieved through relationships. I encourage you to look within yourself, your kinships, and other relations. Kim Tallbear speaks to the importance of relationality within human, animal, nature, and nonhuman. Tallbear also encourages us to decolonize to foster connection in our individualistic culture. It is our communal responsibility as healers to continue our own healing and anti-racist work, so we can foster harm free environments for our clients and students. David Archer says that outside of session, therapists have the

> duty and responsibility to challenge whiteness and concepts of cultural imperialism. Knowing that this comes as a cost, it is necessary for those who seek change to organize and support like-minded individuals for the goal of community and institutional change rather than individual-level adjustments.
>
> (Archer, 2021)

Before we discuss implementation in our clinical work, we will take some time to look at our own self-work and grounding. Overall, I think we could all benefit from slowing down. Some of us got a glimpse of slowing when the COVID-19 pandemic first hit. Others, like myself, did not. Many people, especially healers, worked harder than ever through insurmountable uncertainty. The compounding stress from the global pandemic coupled with the uprisings birthed by the killings of more Black people by police officers changed my work significantly. My work quickly morphed from doing sex therapy with high-functioning clients to crisis interventions and assisting with hospitalizations. All the while feeling like I was working outside of my scope of practice, but showing up for every work day as the consistent factor in my clients' lives, as my own life felt so unclear. We now are seeing the effects of burn out on our mental health and healthcare providers. Many therapists have given more than they had to meet the needs of their community. Collectively, we need rest. Don't let a capitalist-driven grind culture have you overfunctioning or overly ambitious while doing this work. Tricia Hersey writes in *Rest is Resistance: A Manifesto*, "To be colonized is to accept and buy into the lie of our worth being connected to how much we get done" (Hersey, 2022, pp. 21–23). Rest is part of the work. I repeat, rest is part of this work, before you reach your capacity for tolerance, rest.

We need to allow rest for ourselves and others. You are not selfish. You are worthy of slowing down. You are capable of slowing down, just slow down. Whether you're in a white body or a BILPOC body, we all need to rest and to support others in the resistance to be productive or to constantly be doing something. Through this slowing down, we can cultivate the real work that needs to be done. From clarity and choice rather than urgency and confusion, we can move toward freedom—slowing down. Step out of the "urgency" that calls you to do (Menekeem, 2021). I encourage opening up to the possibility of more spaciousness for yourself, your body, and mind, and your community. "Resting is about the beginning process of undoing trauma, so that we can thrive and evolve back to our natural state. A state of ease and rest" (Hersey, 2022, pp. 34–41). Through autocolonization, we have come to believe there is only one way that is "normal" or "right." Be open to the power within. Sometimes, you can only be attuned to it in stillness.

The first steps that I recommend in this work is coming back to the self and body.

Hersey writes:

> Our bodies are a sight of liberation. For us to be more human, returning to
> our natural state before the lies terror and trauma of this system. To be who
> we were before the terror of white supremacy, capitalism, and patriarchy
> is the power of resting. To no longer be ravaged by this culture's incessant
> need to keep going no matter what to produce at all cost. This is why we rest.
>
> (202, 25:51)

Slowing down

At what speed does your body run? Do you feel like you're going fast, slow,
   or somewhere in between?
What speed does your mind run?
Between you mind and your body, which is able to settle the easiest?
What does it look like when you slow down? Is it easy or difficult to slow?
What does it take for you to slow you down?
Think about any pauses you have taken throughout this book?

Remember, you can slow down. Resmaa reminded us in one of our last sessions together that "you have time."

Your nervous system

If your nervous system was a color, what would it be?
Color it if you'd like.
What color is it when it is stressed? What color is it when it is calm?
How are you allowing your nervous system to rest? Give specific examples:

> Learning to settle your body and practicing wise and compassionate self-
> care are not about reducing stress; They're about increasing your body's
> ability to manage stress, as well as about creating more room for your
> nervous system to find coherence and flow.
>
> (Menakem, 2017, p. 152)

Grounding ourselves in our bodies

It's good to check in with yourself every once in a while, to see if you're
   grounded and in your body.
What does it feel like when you are grounded?
What does it feel like when you are not?
What is something that you can do that helps me feel grounded?

What is keeping you from being more grounded in this moment?
What is something I can think or fantasize about that helps you feel grounded?
Some folx benefit from different types of bodywork, such as massage, acupuncture, energy work, and sound healing. Many benefit from movement: dancing, exercising, qigong, yoga, walking, or cuddling.

Breath

Breath is essential to stillness and calm. There are many breath techniques available and easily accessible on the interwebs. However, since this chapter is named for her, I wanted to introduce you to a resource. Carla Tara, the author of *The Oshun Breath: A Breathing Technique for Relaxation, Meditations, and Effective Stress Relief*, defines the Oshun Breath is a "Feminine breath" and continues through a "deep, relaxed, circular breath" Tara goes on to say that "Emotions are energy in motion, and if you stifle them, you can become numb" (p. 14). This book offers steps to "bring you back to your core self, where all wisdom and pleasure reside" (p. 23). When I think about how we translate all of this into clinical work, I think of how when myself or my supervisees have more challenges with countertransference, it's normally when we ourselves are not grounded. This is also a space where therapeutic missteps can happen. It is imperative to stay grounded and to have our nervous systems regulated to do this work.

Another important piece of this examining our own positionality. First and foremost, we need therapeutic connections. If we do not join with the client, we cannot get them very far. Mark and Hause believe, "consideration of the cultural context improves treatment outcomes; moreover, it is essential for ethical care . . . It is crucial for sex therapist to fully understand and to be comfortable with their own social cultural lens prior to working with others" (Mark & Haus, 2020, p. 245). This extends beyond race and culture as Thandiwe Dee Watt-Jones, PhD points out:

> For the therapist of any race to challenge the presence of an "ism" in the room is a matter of inquiry about the client(s)' perspective, how s/he came to that, what experiences, what messages from society taught it, and how does that impact his/her relationship with those targeted by the ism. It is also a matter of the therapist sharing her/his experience of that comment or information s/he might have.
>
> (Thandiwe Dee Watt-Jones, 2016, p 20)

Healing the professional self

Please think about how white privilege shows up in your professional field?
How about cis-hetero-patriarch?
Do you see couple centrism or amatonormativity in your field?

How is race discussed in your field?
How do you discuss race in your work?

Decolonial practice

We cannot avoid examining the complexities of your own biases. Archer writes, "We need to have the courage to bring race into the picture, but only when we ourselves are comfortable confronting our own racial prejudices and hangups" (Archer p. 142). Whatever your race/ethnicity/culture, you have to do the work. White supremacy is insidious, and it's a powerful and sneaky little devil that can show up in our blind spots. When doing the work, be cautious to keep it at a simmer, not a boil. This healing is something that has to take place "slowly over time" (Menekeem, 2020). We are not trying to rush into the scalding fire and allow it to burn us. We need to dip our toe in, tolerate the discomfort, but not allow it to scar us, step back out of it onto sturdy ground, then discern whether or not we want to dip our toe back in. This is a mindfulness practice around the capacity to hold the discomfort. I always tell my clients, "a person can't go to the gym for the very first time and deadlift 300 pounds, right? They have to build up the amount of weight with repetition." You need to find the space that you can tolerate and where your nervous system can stay regulated. Where you can step in and it warms your body, you can hold it, and hold the choice to step out. Sometimes, while doing this work, I went beyond my capacity. I quickly turned to dissociation, and there were a few times that it took me days to feel like I was back to myself. Building awareness around what sensations come up in the body when you are nearing capacity assists with the longevity of the practice.

Sometimes microaggressions or other forms of harm can come from others that cause us to take pause and lick a racialized wound. We could be bracing for this uncomfortable moment to happen or it could come out of the blue with no warning. When we ourselves welcome the exercises that may challenge us and offer the opportunity of self-examination, we are doing something that Resmaa called in our training, "invited reps." These are repetitions of somatic racialized healing that we consensually say "yes" to and choose. Not something that is imposed upon us. Holding discomfort isn't fun. That's why Resmaa cautions us to "build a tolerance for discomfort" (Menkeem, p, 14). I am connected to Resmaa's work because it is grounded in Cultural Somatics, moving us communally to a space of more tolerance.

Archer offers a behavioral path to decolonial practice using the "Five Faces of Oppression" which include decolonizing our vocabulary, our practice, and our actions; promoting equitable practices; donating power and access to others with fewer opportunities; elevating the voices of those who are different from us; and operating from a place of compassion (Archer p. 172). In this, we can "De-link" ourselves of patriarchal, heteronormative, gendered, racist, and couple centric assumptions of coloniality.

In untangling from the patriarchal role, no matter what gender or nongender you are, I encourage you to honor the femininity within you. Honor the matriarchal line that brought us here. Be willing to listen to it within yourself and others.

Sexological systems theory

When we have clients that fall outside the race, gendered, or sexual boundaries, we, as therapists, do an incredible disservice to our clients, if we create an atmosphere where they have to shrink to fit in a box and hide their most authentic parts to accommodate the therapeutic process. Most American therapeutic modalities are, by nature, entrenched with colonial ideologies. To be anti-colonial, one must question the therapeutic training we have received critically to see how our field has worked implicitly and explicitly to uphold amatonormativity, racist-cis-hetero-patriarchy. I have found few models that allow me to break out of therapeutic colonial confines. Due to this, one model that I have grown to appreciate is the "multifactorial approach" sexological systems theory (Jones et al., 2011). The authors too, seeing the limitations of our theories, incorporated Bronfenbrenner's ecological systems theory with their own, sexological systems, to create sexological systems theory. Sexological systems the "sexual relationship is conceptualized as its own systemic structure that interacts along" each of Bronfenbrenner's systems (Jones et al., 2011). This theory was developed to "expand further upon the assessment process" in areas that are seen as a gap in our sexological processes. One of these areas mentioned was the chronosystem of Bronfenbrenner's model. This is looking at changes that happen in a lifespan to ourselves or the environment. In considering sexuality, the chronosystem is what informs the other systems, and I think our American sex history should be considered here. This would assist one in a deeper understanding of clients presenting problems. These two theories have already blended together nicely. However, it is also possible to incorporate the Addressing Model to these concepts by applying it to the sexological system and examining each of the Addressing Model domains throughout the layers of Bronfenbrenner's model. A therapist could also consider their own positionality and how it may be interacting with the client's web of identities and influences.

It is harmful for us, as therapists, to perpetuate colonial harm that we learned as best practices in our training; however, I think the problem becomes more dire when we are working in sexology. This is a field that has fallen victim to colonial ideology and that has had severe consequences in sex therapy. I have not found many theories that allow for the historical pieces mentioned earlier in this text to be incorporated into as our practices in present. Jones et al. (2011) understand the importance of broadening our scope for assessment and treatment. They point out, which many of us already know, a "multifactorial approach to understanding sexuality, a comprehensive explanation for the development of sexuality, all of the psychological factors, life cycle stages and environmental influences, is lacking" (Jones et al., p. 127). With the understanding that "The development of one's sexuality is the result of biological and psychological processes that are enacted within a socio-cultural context, which, in turn, shapes its expression" (Jones et al., 2011, p. 128). It is my suggestion that we include how our history has impacted the "socio-cultural context" of our sexuality. Jones et al. pointed out that therapists have a tendency to conceptualize and treat the "microsystem." This is problematic since, "sexuality can never be separated from current and previous sexual influences and interactions" (Jones, 2011, p. 134). Thus, offering us the invitation to conceptualize our client's sexual relationships, "as its own systemic structure that interacts along with all of the different systems referenced in the (bio)ecological systems theory" (Jones, 2011, p. 134). The beauty of the sexological systems theory is the ability to use it as an assessment, psycho-educational, and intervention tool to "highlight the multi-systemic influences on any person sexuality and sexual relationship" (Jones, 2011, p. 141). This allows us to get to know our clients in a more meaningful way, as we allow them to get to know themselves from a new lens that considers history and the different systems they are a part of. The sexological systems theory offers clients considerations based on a context they had not previously connected to their own suffering or resilience. Jones et al. suggests that when examining these different layers of sexuality, that we bring forward not just the "negative influence" but also the positive ones. "It could prove to be empowering to place an equal, if not higher, focus on the positive experiences" (Jones, 2011, p. 138).

Clinical strategies

Invite the calm into the therapeutic space.
Be curious.
Get consent prior to implementing interventions or initiating difficult discussions.
Invite conversations of colonial concepts such as patriarchy, cis-heteronormativity, racism, ableism.
Encourage alternative healing modalities.
Support cultural, spiritual, and linguistic revitalization.
Promote Afro-centered and Afro-inspired resources like Afrosexolgy.
Encourage clean eating and hydration: our bodies need to be nourished to carry our mental health.
Use of music in session and as homework.
Interventions that allow for the ritual to connect with self, others, animals, environment, and/or planet.

Tenants of ecosexuality can be implemented to connect to the earth. At minimum, getting outside can help cleanse the stagnant energy that accumulate doing this work.

Allow for ancestors to be acknowledged in the therapeutic space.

White therapist working with Black folx

Reflect on the following questions:

Do you ask your clients how they identify their race on your intake paperwork?
If so, is it a box that they check or can they write it in themselves?
During the intake, do you discuss race? If so, how do you bring it up?
Do you bring up your racial difference and assess how the client feels about the difference?
What are some ways you can begin to have deeper conversations around ethnosexuality?

Recommendations

Ask for permission to discuss race with the client.
Only proceed after getting consent.
Disclosure the parts of your positionality that you feel appropriate to share.
Discuss your limitations (use the Expanded Addressing Model).
Ask about the client's previous experience with white providers.
Seek clinical supervision.

Supervisors

Another supporting and brilliant mentor of mine is one of the editors for this publication, and one of the editors in our book, *An Intersectional Approach to Sex Therapy*, and this publication, James Wadley writes in his chapter of the book,

> Given the painful history of slavery, segregation, Jim Crow laws, health disparities, stereotypes and myths, and racist rhetoric, there are a myriad of trauma-related challenges that may be obstructions to talking and listening about racial related issues in non-professional and professional spaces. When race is tied with the taboo subject of sexuality, it seems even more difficult to address how it may be woven into supervisor and supervisee identities and therapeutic decision-making.
>
> (Wadley, 2022, p. 26)

It is important that the supervisor "do their own work" and bring their individual work into their own racial communities prior to engaging in dialogue with others outside of their race. Practice with your own people. When establishing the supervisory relationship, it is our responsibility as supervisors and mentors to encourage cultural exploration with treatment and conceptualization. It is important for us to open these discussions early in our work with the supervisee. Hardy and Bobes (2016) recommend that you initiate these conversations "No later than the second session, to set the tone to explicitly acknowledge and validate the lived experience of group members of diverse backgrounds." In that, it helps to disclose your own social location to your supervisees and mentees. Additionally, "Provide resources to supervisees and mentees where they can learn from people of color and other marginalized voices" (Hardy & Bobes, 2016). However, do not expect BILPOC people to do the labor of educating without compensation. Thandiwe Dee Watt-Jones, PhD writes,

> For many, having a therapist who recognizes their experiences with oppression can be a relieving and assuring. For supervisees of color, it can be encouraging that the supervision can mirror their experience of how race/racism impacts them as therapists as well as clients.
> (Thandiwe Dee Watt-Jones, 2016, p. 19)

To end, I would like to draw on hooks one last time. She writes, "To heal our wounded communities, which are diverse and multi-layered, we must return to a love ethic, one that is exemplified by the combined forces of care, respect, knowledge, and responsibility" (Hooks, 2001, p. 4).

Something I learned while studying with Resmaa was that communal healing is imperative. Racialized sexual trauma is something that we need to heal from communally, standing in solidarity with others that are committed to doing similar work. We need people of all ages, races, and positionalities to be here for our collective healing. We aren't just doing it for us. The work you do now is a gift and a shift for future generations. It is our responsibility as future mental health ancestors to re-exist.

References

Alvarez, A. (2014). *Native America and the question of genocide*. Rowman & Littlefield.

Archer, D. (2021) *Anti-Racist Psychotherapy: Confronting systemic racism and healing racial trauma*. Each One Teach One Publications.

Baptist, E. E. (2014). *The half has never been told: Slavery and the making of American capitalism*. Basic Books.

Berry, D. R., & Harris, L. M. (2018). *Sexuality and slavery: Reclaiming intimate histories in the Americas*. The University of Georgia Press.

Brake, E., (2012), *Minimizing Marriage: Marriage, Morality, and the Law*, Oxford: Oxford University Press, ISBN 978-0-19-977414-2

Brake, E. (2012). Amatonormativity. *ElizabethBrake.com*. https://elizabethbrake.com/amatonormativity/

Buggery Act 1533. (2021, December, 21). *In wikipedia*. https://en.wikipedia.org/wiki/Buggery_Act_1533#cite_note-2

Burke, T. (2019, January 4). Me Too is a Movement, Not a Moment [Video]. YouTube. URL https://youtu.be/zP3LaAYzA3Q.

D'Emilio, J., & Freedman, E. B. (2012). *Intimate matters: A history of sexuality in America*. The University of Chicago Press.

DiAngelo, R. J. (2012) *What Does it Mean to Be White?: Developing White Racial Literacy*. Peter Lang.

Degruy, J. (2005, 2017). *Post traumatic slave syndrome: America's legacy of enduring injury and healing*. Joy DeGruy Publications Inc.

Fielding, L. (2021). *Trans sex: Clinical approaches to trans sexualities and erotic embodiments*. Routledge.

Foster, T. A. (2014). The sexual abuse of black men under American slavery. In D. R Berry, & L. M. Harris (Eds.), *Sexuality & slavery: Reclaiming intimate histories in the Americas* (pp. 124–144). University of Georgia Press.

Foster, T. A., (2018). The Sexual Abuse of Black Men Under American Slavery. In D. R. Berry & L. M. Harris, Sexuality & Slavery: Reclaiming Intimate Histories in the Americas. (pp. 124–144). The University of Georgia Press.

Giddens, R. [NPR Music]. (2019, September 23). *Rhiannon Giddens: NPR Music Tiny Desk Concert*. [Video]. YouTube. https://youtu.be/q0fIdFx3pbY

Gilbert, T. Q. (2022). *Black and sexy: A framework of racialized sexuality*. Routledge.

Hardy, K. V., & Bobes, T. (2016). Core competencies for executing culturally sensitive supervision and training. In *Culturally sensitive supervision and training: Diverse perspectives and practical applications* (pp. 11–15). Routledge.

Hart & Rennison. (2003). Bureau of Justice Statistics Special Report. U.S. Department of Justice.

Hays, P. (2001). *Addressing cultural complexities in practice*. Washington, DC: American Psychological Association.

Hays, P. (2008). *Addressing cultural complexities in practice*. Washington, DC: American Psychological Association.

Hepworth Clark, Z. S. (2015). *Coming to my senses: A decolonizing autoethnographic exploration of osunality*. [Doctoral dissertation], Widener University. www.zelaika.com/contact

Hersey, T. (2022). Rest is Resistance: A Manifesto. (T. Hersey, Narr.) [Audiobook]. Audible.com. https://www.audible.com/pd/Rest-Is-Resistance-Audiobook/B09W6BG48H (Original work publish 2022)

Hooks, B. (2001). *Salvation: Black people and love*. HarperCollins.

Iantaffi, A., (2021). *Gender Trauma: Healing cultural, social, and historical gendered trauma*. Jessica Kingsley Publishers.

Jones, K. E., Meneses da Silva, A. M., & Soloski, K. L. (2011). Sexological systems theory: An ecological model and assessment approach for sex therapy. *Sexual and Relationship Therapy, 26*(2), 127–144. https://doi.org10.1080/14681994.2011.574688

Jones-Rogers, S. E. (2019). *They were her property: White women as slave owners in the American South*. Yale University Press.

Kort, J. (2018). *LGBTQ clients in therapy: Clinical issues and treatment strategies*. W.W. Norton & Company.

Livingston, G., & Brown, A. (2017, May 18). Trends and patterns in intermarriage. *PEW Research Center*. www.pewresearch.org/social-trends/2017/05/18/1-trends-and-patterns-in-intermarriage/

Malone, R. M., Stewart, M. R., Gary-Smith, M., & Wadley, J. C. (2022). *An Intersectional Approac to Sex Therapy: Centering the Lives of Black, Indigenous, racialized, and People of Color*. (Malone, R. M., Stewart, M. R., Gary-Smith, M., & Wadley, J. C.). Routledge

Mark, K., & Haus, K. (2020). Culture and sexuality. In K. M. Hertlien, N. Gambescia, & G. R. Weeks (Eds.), *Systemic sex therapy* (pp. 245–257) Routledge.

Me Too Movement. (2018, April 10). This is the 'me too movement'. *YouTube* https://www.youtube.com/watch?v=ZF55ItXWjck.

Menakem, R. (2017). My grandmother's hands: Racialized trauma and the pathway to mending our heart and body. In *Central recovery press. Reviewed by: Catharine Roslyn Stimpson, New York University School of Arts and Science Central Recovery Press*. https://doi.org/10.1177/0361684319879761

Menekeem, R. (2020). Somatic Medicine and COVID-19: Webinar for Healers of Color [Webinar]. University of Washington Counseling Center.

Menekeem, R. (2021). *Communal Consultation for Black Bodies*. Education for Racial Equity.

Mignolo, W. D. (2016). Forward: Decolonial body-geo-politics at large. In *Decolonizing Sexualities: Transnational perspectives critical interventions*. Counterpress.

Nagel, N. (2000). Ethnicity and sexuality. *Annual Review of Sociology, 26*, 107–133. www.jstor.org/stable/223439

Nzegwu, N. (2011). Osunality (or African eroticism). In S. Tamale (Ed.), *African sexualities* (pp. 253–270). Pambazuka Press.

Oluo, I. (2021). *Whipped for lying with a black woman* (I. X Kendi & K. N. Blain, Eds.). One World

Oshodi, J. E. (2004). *Back then and right now in the history of psychology: A history of Human Psychology in African perspectives for the new millennium.* AuthorHouse.

Perry, I. (2018) *Vexing Thing: On gender and liberation.* Duke University Press.

Race and Sexuality. (2022, September 3). *In Wikipedia.* https://en.wikipedia.org/wiki/Race_and_sexuality#cite_note-24

Solomon, R. (2017). Sexual practice and fantasy in Colonial America and the early republic. *IU Journal of Undergraduate Research, 3*(1), 24–35. https://doi.org/10.14434/iujur.v3i1.23364

Stimpson, C. R. (2020). Book Review: Darkness now visible: Patriarchy's resurgence and feminist resistance; Why does patriarchy persist? *Psychology of Women Quarterly, 44*(1), 139–140. https://doi.org/10.1177/0361684319879761

TED. (2020, August 11). *Hetero-patriarchy and Settler Colonialism. | Reid Gustafson* [Video]. YouTube. https://youtu.be/-wRbfOmHgts

Thandiwe Dee Watts, J. (2016). Location of self in training and supervision. In *Culturally sensitive supervision and training: Diverse perspectives and practical applications* (pp. 16–24). Routledge.

The Expanded Addressing Model. (Hays, 2001). Chart is based on materials from Leticia Nieto, Psy.D., St. Martin's University, Lacey, WA. Other contributors of descriptors: Kamuela Ka'Ahanui, Ph.D., Center for Programs in Education, Antioch University Seattle (race and dogma) (K. Ka'Ahanui, personal communication, February 9, 2006); Katherine Aubrey, MA, graduate of Antioch University Seattle (b-iracial and adoption status) (K. Aubrey, personal communication September 9, 2007); Jen Jackson Crum, graduate student at Antioch University Seattle (multiracial) (J. Crum, personal communication, September 9, 2008); relational; regional (Blake, September, 2008); genetics: fostering (A. Blake, November, 2009); trauma (A. Blake, February 6, 2009); giftedness (L. Erickson, May 1, 2012).

Treatment of Slaves in the United States. (2022, June 26). *In Wikipedia.* https://en.wikipedia.org/wiki/Treatment_of_slaves_in_the_United_States#Rape_and_sexual_abuse

Urban Indian Health Institute. (2022). *Urban Indian Health.* www.uihi.org/

Wadley, J. C. (2022). *Black Like Me: Reflections from a Black Male Sex Therapist and Supervisor.* In R. M. Malone, M. R. Steward & J. C. Wadley (Eds,), *An Intersectional Approach to Sex Therapy: Centering the Lives of Black, Indigenous, racialized, and People of Color. (pp. 25–34). Routledge*

Wilkerson, I. (2020). *Caste: The origins of our discontents.* New York, NY: Random House.

Wriggins, J. (1983). Faculty scholarship at University of Maine School of Law Digital Commons. *Digital Commons.* https://digitalcommons.mainelaw.maine.edu/cgi/viewcontent.cgi?article=1042&context=faculty-publications

Index